S0-AGO-639

THE *Speedwell* VOYAGE

THE *Speedwell* VOYAGE

A Tale of Piracy and Mutiny in the Eighteenth Century

Kenneth Poolman

Naval Institute Press
Annapolis, Maryland

Library of Congress Cataloging-in-Publication Data

Poolman, Kenneth, 1924–
The Speedwell voyage : a tale of piracy and mutiny in the eighteenth century / Kenneth Poolman.
p. cm.
Includes bibliographical references and index.
ISBN 1-55750-693-0 (alk. paper)
1. Speedwell (Ship)—History—18th century. 2. Shelvocke, George. 3. Voyages around the world—History—18th century. 4. Pirates—Great Britain—Biography. I. Title.
G420.S65P66 1999
910.4′1—dc21 98-42419

Printed in the United States of America on acid-free paper ∞

99 00 01 02 03 04 05 06 9 8 7 6 5 4 3 2

First printing

To the destructive element submit yourself,
and with the exertion of your hands and feet in the
water make the deep, deep sea keep you up.

JOSEPH CONRAD, *Lord Jim*

Contents

Acknowledgments

For their kind and expert help with research for this book, I wish to thank Iain MacKenzie and Brian Duncan Thynne of the National Maritime Museum, Greenwich, London; and Jenny Wraight, Admiral Librarian, Ministry of Defence, London.

THE *Speedwell* VOYAGE

Geography of Shelvocke's voyage.

Realms of Silver

WIDELY INFAMOUS throughout the Royal Navy from the seventeenth to the early nineteenth centuries was the figure of the corrupt purser. "A Navy purser," wrote diarist and Secretary of the Navy Samuel Pepys, "knows how to transmute rotten peas and mouldy oätmeal into pure gold and silver and purse up roundly for himself from the wages of dead tarpaulins . . . a purser without professed cheating is a professed loser."[1] The particularly notorious purser Andrew Miller gave his name to the whole service, and it is still known familiarly today as the Andrew.[2]

One such was Edward Hughes, a former naval clerk at Portsmouth, who by 1718 had a thriving business in "the City" of London, a country mansion, and a wealthy wife.[3]

One of Hughes's enterprises in which he was the principal partner was the Gentlemen Adventurers' Association. The name evoked memories of the old Merchant Venturers' company of London and Bristol, which had backed the Cabots' voyages to the New World, but there were no gentlemen on *this* board. It was a shady outfit.

The European political situation had given Hughes and his partners, merchants Henry Neale and Beake Winder and Barbary trader John Gumley, an idea for a new commercial gamble.[4]

In the War of the Spanish Succession (1701–13), England and her old enemy Holland had supported the Austrian empire in its struggle against France for possession of Spain, the latter's American colonies, and the Spanish Netherlands. After twelve years of attrition, French power lay broken on land and sea, Spain was ravaged by profitless fighting, and Austria was bankrupt.[5]

At the Congress of Utrecht in 1713, Britain masterminded a fresh balance of power underwritten by the new Quadruple Alliance, comprising Austria, Great Britain, Holland, and their late enemy, France. Both the Bourbon monarchy of France and the Austrian house of Hapsburg had family claims upon the Spanish empire. Following the will of the Spanish king Charles II, Spain and her American colonies were assigned to the French Philip of Anjou, Louis XIV's grandson, as Philip V of Spain. The disputed territories of the Spanish Netherlands, Naples and Sardinia, went to Austria, while Sicily went to the Duchy of Savoy, Austria's southern ally.

As a sop to Spain, the family of the Spanish queen, Elizabeth Farnese of Parma, was graciously permitted to retain her Italian duchy with the addition of Tuscany.

To the fiery Elizabeth, already caught up in emerging Spanish nationalist fervor, this was an insult. She redoubled her support of the Spanish éminence grise, Cardinal Alberoni, her Parma countryman, who was masterminding a revolt.

Austria was still fighting a drawn-out war against Turkey, France was exhausted by fighting, Britain was preoccupied with threatened invasion by forces backing the restoration of the Jacobite Catholic kings. Holland, which valued its trade with Spain, was a lukewarm member of the Quadruple Alliance. Alberoni saw his chance.

In 1717 Spanish forces recaptured Sardinia. In July 1718, Sicily was attacked. War with the Quadruple Alliance seemed inevitable. In London, Edward Hughes and his Gentlemen Adventurers saw an opportunity to fit out a small squadron of privateering vessels, licensed by the crown, to prey on Spanish treasure houses and ships on the Pacific coast of the Americas.

As a trading tycoon with a naval background and contacts, Hughes knew more than most of his peers of the lucrative expeditions to the Pacific of William Dampier and Woodes Rogers. For well over a century, since the days of Francis Drake, Spanish-American waters had been the hunting grounds for English privateers and pirates. They were still realms of silver, if not gold, in the eyes of London merchants. Rogers, in this very spring of 1718, was on his way out to the Bahamas, which he had been renting for twenty-one years as governor with some of the proceeds from his 1707 voyage to the South Sea.

William Dampier, son of a tenant farmer of East Coker, near Yeovil, Somerset, had preceded him.

As a child, Dampier was bright, not cut out to be a farmhand. His father died when he was ten, but he continued at the grammar school, spoiled by his mother until she died six years later. He was then forced to leave school and look for work. An impulse took him to sea before the mast, in a voyage from Weymouth to Newfoundland. When war broke out with Holland in 1672,[6] Dampier served as an able seaman in His Majesty's Ship *Royal Prince.*[7] Later, as manager of a plantation in Jamaica, he had no aptitude for the job, grew bored, and shipped out with a buccaneer. But the sailing master was incompetent, and Dampier took over the navigation. He soon mastered it, along with acquiring a good knowledge of pilotage and hydrography. He returned to England in 1678 a rich man and married into the wealthy Grafton family.

But the buccaneer's life still called him. In 1679 he joined the Sharpe-Sawkins band of hard cases. With them, he crossed the Isthmus of Panama and helped sack Santa Maria.

By 1688 Dampier was commanding his own ship, but he could not handle his roughneck ship's company, who marooned him on

Great Nicobar Island, north of Sumatra. He escaped in a canoe and returned to England with a tattooed Manargis islander, whom he exhibited as an "Indian prince."

In 1697 he published his hydrographical discoveries in *Voyage Round the World,* and, in 1699, in *A Discourse on Winds.* The success of these works gained him command of the *Roebuck* and an expedition to explore and chart Terra Australia. He made an expert survey of the coasts but neglected his captain's duties, and the discontent of the crew drove him to drink. Back home, Dampier was found guilty of harsh conduct and unfit to be employed as commander of any of His Majesty's ships. Before long, however, he was being introduced to the queen by the Lord High Admiral as leader of a new expedition. He sailed on 16 April 1703 in the twenty-six-gun privateer *St. George,* in company with the sixteen-gun galley *Cinque Ports,* their real objective the South Sea. He fell out with his crew, drank heavily, and abused his officers. There were frequent mutinies. Alexander Selkirk, the Scottish sailing master of the *Cinque Ports* who had quarreled violently with his captain, "Bully" Stradling, was marooned on Juan Fernandez (Mas a Tierra) Island, four hundred miles off the coast of Chile.[8]

Attacks on a "Manila galleon," carrying silver to exchange for rich Chinese merchandise in the Philippines, and on a French ship were repelled with heavy losses. Unable to get another command, in 1707 Dampier was lucky to be given the billet of sailing master in the *Duke,* flagship of Woodes Rogers, which, with the *Duchess,* was bound for the South Sea on a marauding cruise.

Rogers maintained discipline among his ship's company of "sailors, tinkers, pedlars, fiddlers and haymakers" by making a troublemaker's best mate or "winger" flog him—his method, too, of breaking any "unlawful friendship."[9] By 31 January 1709, they were off Juan Fernandez. As they approached the island in the darkness, they saw a light ashore; in the morning, they brought off Alexander Selkirk.[10]

Then Rogers captured a Spanish ship from Manila loaded with a valuable cargo of Chinese goods, and he was back home on 1 October 1711, with treasure worth two hundred thousand pounds, a huge fortune in those days (ten million today). It was not distributed for some years, and Dampier died in 1714, without having seen any of his share.

Meanwhile, Rogers had published *A Cruising Voyage Round the World.* Among the many who bought copies were the Gentlemen Adventurers, Hughes, Neale, Winder, and Gumley. For a long time they failed to find the right sort of man to command their South Sea foray—not too scrupulous but a good seaman, with the sort of leadership qualities that had made Woodes Rogers so successful and had been so conspicuously lacking in Will Dampier.

It was at this point that George Shelvocke, an old shipmate of Edward Hughes's, called upon him.

There were parallels between Shelvocke and Dampier. The Shelvocke family of Deptford, below London on the river Thames, were farmers from Shropshire turned mariners. George was born in 1675 and joined the Royal Navy as a boy seaman when he was fifteen. He was in time for service in two long wars against France and Spain.[11] Both conflicts featured much storm-tossed seatime and gritty action.

War brings promotion—or death. Young George studied navigation, won his Trinity House certificate as an English Channel pilot, and, in March 1703, was given the king's warrant as sailing master (navigating officer) of the frigate His Majesty's Ship *Scarborough,* thirty-two guns. The ship's purser was Edward Hughes. The two men became chaffing friends, though different as chalk and cheese. A year later, in April 1704, Shelvocke was granted an acting commission as lieutenant in the same ship, confirmed in November 1705. He was then appointed third lieutenant of the ninety-gun *Association,* flagship of Rear Admiral Sir Thomas Dilkes, in January 1706. In August Dilkes shifted his flag to the *Britannia,* taking all his officers with him.

Britannia paid off at Chatham in October, and George Shelvocke's career took a different turn. Until then he had advanced steadily toward command and had become second lieutenant of a flagship. But he could not now get another commission. In July 1707 he shipped as purser of the *Monck,* sixty guns. It was a drop in status. A purser was one of a ship's "standing officer" specialists, along with the sailing master and gunner, all of whom had lost authority with the creation of lieutenants in the days of Drake and the armada, though the job had its compensations.

Shelvocke stayed in the job for six years, until 1713, when war with France ended. Many officers, including Shelvocke, were beached, with only a few senior officers allowed even half pay ashore. In five years Shelvocke, whose wife, Susannah, daughter of a Navy captain, had died in 1711, and his son, George, were living in poverty.

In the depths of depression, Shelvocke ran into Edward Hughes, who invited him down to his elegant country house. Hughes noted that although his old shipmate was gaunt and pale-cheeked, his back was as straight as ever and his clothes, worn and threadbare, were clean. His weathered shoes were properly soled and heeled, buckles polished. He was still, to all appearances, Lieutenant Shelvocke, shipshape and Bristol fashion.

They reminisced over glasses of sherry, with Shelvocke noting the signs of prosperity—walls draped in roseate silk, gleaming nut-brown side tables, silver-set decanters—and Hughes waiting for the beached mariner to make his embarrassed pitch. Finally Shelvocke told him that he and young George Junior literally "had no bread to eat and not a friend in the world from whom I can expect any help, saving your good self."[12]

Hughes thought he had probably found his commander for the South Sea enterprise. Shelvocke, he guessed, was a true-blue, still, at heart. That would be to their advantage, as it would make him a company man. That he had seen the view from the scuppers as well as the maintop should, however, make him somewhat less scrupulous in terms of niceties in the prosecution of their interests. His professional qualifications spoke for themselves: ten years before the mast, qualified pilot, expert sailing master, a decade commanding a watch. . . . The combination was rare and fitted their specifications well. What rust had gathered on George Shelvocke's sextant a brisk sou'westerly would soon scour. George on dry land was like a lobster out of water.

Hughes outlined his plan for the new expedition. Shelvocke said that he would sign on as a boatswain's (bosun's) mate if necessary. When told that he was being offered command, a commodore's billet, he was shocked speechless, and tears came to his eyes. Hughes gave him a twenty-pound note in advance of his pay and sent him off to supervise the fitting out and manning of the ships.

The Adventurers' squadron was to comprise two ships, the 350-ton, thirty-six-gun *Success* and the 200-ton twenty-two-gun *Speedwell*. Shelvocke would command the squadron in the *Speedwell*, with Capt. John Clipperton in command of the *Success*.[13] Clipperton had made two previous voyages to the Pacific coast of the Americas and had been chief mate in Dampier's *St. George*, but he had an unsavory reputation.

While the *St. George* had been refitting in the Gulf of Nicoy (Nicoya), Costa Rica, he and Dampier, both volatile men, had quarreled. On 2 September 1704, Clipperton, with twenty men, had seized a ten-ton, two-masted prize barque, and departed on a buccaneering voyage of his own.

The barque was carrying all of Dampier's ammunition and most of his provisions. Clipperton landed most of the latter on an island and sent word to Dampier. He left himself two swivel guns, two or three barrels of powder, and some shot. In the Rio Leon on the Mexican coast, he took two prizes. One sank, the other was ransomed for four thousand dollars. In the bay of Salinas, the ship was drawn up on shore, cleaned, and refitted. Clipperton then sailed for the East Indies, reaching the Philippines in fifty-four days. Here he held a Spanish priest as hostage for provisions and water. Thence he sailed to Macao, where his crew split up. Some joined the East India Company in Bengal, some the Portuguese in Goa, others the service of the Great Mogul. Clipperton himself returned to England in 1706. The reputation that had disqualified him in the eyes of more scrupulous potential employers actually recommended him to Hughes.

In the autumn of 1718, Britain was not officially a belligerent. To become privateers, Shelvocke's two ships were to fly the flag of the emperor Charles VI of Austria, which was at war with Spain.

Shelvocke sailed in the *Speedwell* to Ostend in Belgium, which was part of the Austrian empire, to obtain privateer commissions from the emperor and lay in a stock of wines and spirits. The ship's name was changed to *Starhemburg* for service under the Austrian flag. The *Success* became the *Prince Eugene.*

Shelvocke, however, was given strict orders not to fire any guns or hoist any colors yet. He was to take aboard no more than sixty Flemish seamen and three officers, any shortfall to be made up from what he could scrape up in English ports. With him he took George Junior, and his nephew Will Adams as ship's surgeon.

When Hughes, Neale, and Winder went out to the Downs anchorage off the Kent coast in southwest England in November, they expected to find both their ships there. The *Success* was swinging round her hook, but the absence of the *Speedwell/Starhemburg* made them uneasy.

When she did come in at the end of the first week in December, they learned that Shelvocke had disobeyed their orders on several points. He had got the commissions, but at the price of signing on ninety-six Flemish subjects of the emperor, including six officers. He had fired away five barrels of powder and made deep inroads into the stock of wine and brandy, embarked for the use of both ships, in lavish entertaining. With the imperial colors hoisted, the truculent Flemings had treated the ship as their property. To some of the British jack-tars, it looked as if they intended to take her over. Hughes began to fear that the old incorruptible Shelvocke had, after all, been eroded by the grim years of hand-to-mouth.

Command of the venture was transferred from Shelvocke to Clipperton. Shelvocke's consequent humiliation increased the dislike and mistrust that he already felt for the former buccaneer, who actually boasted of his days with the brilliant but disreputable Dampier. But to oppose the new arrangement would have meant dismissal and poverty again. Clipperton took command of the squadron in the *Success/Prince Eugene,* while Shelvocke remained in the *Speedwell/Starhemburg.*

Desperate diplomatic efforts by British prime minister Stanhope in Madrid had failed to avert war. While the two ships were still in the Downs, Great Britain declared war on Spain, and the two Austrian names were dropped. The owners paid off Shelvocke's arrogant Flemings, and Hughes applied for British letters of marque for Clipperton and Shelvocke. Both captains were given copies of Woodes Rogers's *Cruising Voyage Round the World.*

Thanks largely to Shelvocke's delay in Belgium, the expedition was already late in leaving Britain. According to the Adventurers' instructions, the two ships should have cleared the English Channel in mid-November 1718. This would have given them three months to get into the Straits of Magellan at Cape Horn, where they were to take on wood and clean their bottoms, to be in the South Sea by the beginning of February 1719.

In 1519 Magellan had used the southern trades to make the first European crossing of the Pacific. Four subsequent successive expeditions, led by Loiasa, Saavedra, Grijalva, and Villalobos, suffered death and disaster and failed to find a return passage to the Americas. A survivor of Loiasa's squadron was the young Andres de Urdaneta. When another expedition sailed in 1564 to colonize the Philippines and search for a return route, Urdaneta, who had since taken holy orders, was the effective leader. Arellano's small, forty-ton, *San Lucas* lost the main fleet and wandered north to Japan, by sheer chance caught the westerly winds and an eastern-flowing current, and reached America in July 1565. Urdaneta, who had actually planned a similar route, sailed north from the Philippines, picked up the westerlies and the California current, and reached home on 18 September.

Spanish ships followed him, to trade Peruvian silver for rich Chinese merchandise at Cavite, near Manila. Urdaneta's precisely charted route was used by all vessels until the English captain Cook updated it in 1771.

The Adventurers' prime target had been the king of Spain's ship leaving Acapulco for Cavite in the spring of 1719, with Peruvian silver to pay for cargoes of Chinese silks, Oriental furniture, and wonderful objets d'art in sandalwood, porcelain, ivory, jade, and gold. In the past the Spanish silver had gone to help finance the building of China's Great Wall.

If Clipperton and Shelvocke missed the king's ship this time, they were to try to take the island of Puna and the town of Guayaquil, previously sacked by Woodes Rogers. Here there were, according to Rogers, seldom less than three million dollars in the king's warehouse. Other targets were Payta and Collan in the southeast, about 150 leagues from Guayaquil.

They should clean ship, Clipperton advised, at the Tres Marias Islands on the coast of Mexico, or in the Gulf of Nicoraga (Nicaragua). There they could collect wood and water, and victual with turtle meat. Then, according to the original plan, they would sail to Acapulco, lie eight leagues off the land, capture the next treasure ship, then cross the Pacific and Indian oceans to Mauritius, watering at Guam in the Mariana Islands if necessary. If this attack was not possible, they should be off Acapulco in the following February, 1720, before the first outward-bound silver galleon sailed that year.

This plan had been masterminded by Hughes, with Dampier's account of his South Sea voyage and Woodes Rogers's book at his elbow. To make it work, one factor was vital: In ships so far from home, with little chance of help or rescue, leadership was all-important. Such an expedition could succeed or fail by the strengths and weaknesses of its commander. That fine seamanship mattered went without saying. Equally important was the overall commander's ability to manage men, in this case two ships' companies of illiterate, superstitious sailors, sullen landsmen, jail scrapings, gallow's meat, and malcontents, needing only a common grievance, real or imaginary, and the machinations of some "sea lawyer" to touch off mutiny.

Magellan and Drake had been such men. But, brilliant navigator, explorer, and cartographer though he was, Will Dampier was not. Lacking the Somerset man's intellectual abilities, Woodes Rogers left technicalities to his specialists—gunnery to the gunner, discipline to the bosun, navigation to sailing master Dampier. Rogers knew men, especially British tarpaulins and their simplistic psychology. He held his crews together with a consistent blend of harshness and commonsense tolerance that gained their respect and trust.

Through unanticipated intemperance and rashness, Shelvocke, the former Navy officer, had lost command of the Adventurers' squadron to the ex-buccaneer Clipperton, the devious, unstable, and untrustworthy.

Shelvocke was still in command of a ship. Originally the true-blue tar who had risen to a position of authority by skill and conduct, it remained to be seen just how much the hole-in-corner existence that had followed his beaching and his experience in the venal billet of purser had influenced him. His first essay in command had not been encouraging. The voyage of the *Speedwell,* high seas privateer, would encompass greed, envy, tyranny, class hatred, and a crude socialism. Above all it would be about command—its demands, its limitations, its proper application in a ship and perhaps, by extension, in the wider world.

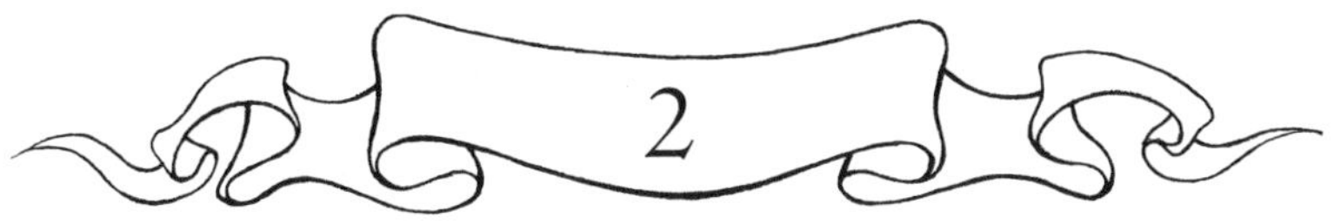

2

Crank and Tender

THE FRICTION that had developed between Shelvocke and Clipperton caused further delays in sailing. Shelvocke, especially after a few jars of wine, made pointed contrasts between his own Royal Navy background, in his opinion the only nursery for sea officers, and that of the commodore. He belittled Clipperton as a tradesman and a freebooter. All this filtered through to the *Success.* Shelvocke's public tirades against the change of command became so frequent that the whole ship's company took sides.

Finally the scuttlebutt reached London. Hughes wrote to Shelvocke deploring his near-mutinous conduct and rudeness to Clipperton, warning him that if he did not receive by return of post the firm assurance that he was content with his present appointment, he would be replaced.

Shelvocke realized that he had gone too far. On 19 December, fearful at the idea of being thrown on the streets again, he wrote to Hughes, "All resentments are laid aside by me long since, and don't doubt brotherhood with Captain Clipperton."[1]

The two ships sailed for Plymouth, where they were delayed for several weeks waiting for a suitable wind. During this time they topped up their crews, mostly from dockside riffraff. Shelvocke's sea legs had quickly returned, though he found the *Speedwell* top-heavy. By a mistake in the loading, she was carrying the bulk of the expedition's alcohol, while the *Success* had all the tobacco.

These extra burdens, added to the weight of a first command, were made the heavier by having to subordinate himself to a superior he considered devious, untrustworthy, and incompetent. Clipperton was also unpopular with his own officers, who had to suffer foulmouthed abuse during the commodore's frequent bouts of violent drunkenness. Yet Clipperton had the company's ear, which deepened Shelvocke's feelings of being manipulated by Hughes and his dubious Gentlemen Adventurers, whose only "adventure" was financial. Beggars couldn't be choosers, Hughes had seen that quickly enough, but they had got him cheap, and he would make sure to purse up for himself.

At last, on 13 February 1719, the winds were propitious, and Clipperton's little squadron put out into the lively Western Approaches. Two days into the angry Atlantic, *Speedwell* came under *Success*'s lee, and Shelvocke shouted through his speaking trumpet: "Sir, my ship is very crank. She carries too much aloft. You must send for your part of the wine and brandy so that I may stow some of my guns below and redress the balance and hold with you." Clipperton did not reply.[2]

There followed twenty-four hours of fresh gales and lashing rain. That evening Clipperton was forced to shorten sail several times to stay with *Speedwell,* and the two ships kept company until the night of 19 February, when, between nine and ten o'clock, an exceptionally wild wind blew out of the southwest. Shelvocke was forced to take in his topsails.

The fury of the gale increased, Clipperton made the signal for bringing to, and Shelvocke hauled up his foresail to come under Clipperton's lee. But contact was impossible, and by eleven o'clock the two ships lay some way apart, *Speedwell,* under bare poles, with her sails "a portland" (lowered to the level of the gunwale) and unable to suffer a single knot of canvas all night except, briefly, a reefed mizzen.

"At last the winds were propitious." (Ministry of Defence, England)

About midnight a sea struck *Speedwell* on her quarter and smashed in one of her quarter and one of her big stern deadlights, through which the sea poured until they could be temporarily stopped up again. Most of the crew, especially the wretched landsmen who formed four-fifths of the ship's company, were either certain that the ship was about to founder or too seasick to care. Shelvocke could not get the ship before the wind or work her ordinary pumps, the lee pump being underwater, with prodigious seas driving over them and knocking down any man foolish enough to stand upright.

The owners had grumbled at the cost of a chain pump, uncommon in a ship of only two hundred tons, but Shelvocke had insisted on having one fitted. This now saved them from going under, though the "crank" *Speedwell* was still in some danger. In the end the only damage permanently sustained was the spoiling of about ten hundredweight of bread and one barrel of powder.

By the forenoon of 20 February, the gale had abated somewhat. At two o'clock in the afternoon, *Success* wore and made sail, steering away south-by-east, but Shelvocke made no speed to follow her. At noon *Speedwell* set her mainsail, double-reefed, and, at midnight, set topsails and stood to the northwest.

Next day a large piece of wreckage bumped alongside. After examining it Shelvocke pronounced it part of the *Success,* which, he said, although a speedy sailer, was built very light, and she was overstored, and the weight of her metal had torn her sides out. Shortly after this, Shelvocke was informed that some seventy of his crew had been so terrified by the storm that they thought the ship too crank to be able to carry them to the South Seas, and they were demanding that she be turned about and sailed back to England. On 23 February, he ordered all the hands on deck and tried to allay the men's fears.

If the ship was truly crank and tender owing to her being pestered so much aloft, in a little time, Shelvocke assured them, they would eat and drink her into a lighter and better trim. This raised a half-hearted laugh from some of the men. When the quarter and great cabin lights were boarded up with good strong planks and an awning made to shelter those on deck from the rain and breaking waves, the ship would be ready to face the voyage that would make them all rich men. A small spirit of wind would soon bring fair weather.

But the men were not convinced, and they continued to demand that the helm be put aweather to bring the ship before the wind and return home. They became so threatening that Shelvocke armed all the officers, who paraded on deck. The would-be mutineers dispersed.

Shelvocke took the opportunity to seize two of the ringleaders and lash them to the jeers for punishment with the cat. But some of the others begged him to pardon them and promised to behave obediently in future. Shelvocke gave way, ordered up the brandy, and they all drank to a prosperous voyage. He found that a few drams at the right time proved the best medicine for allaying fears and suppressing mutinous urges and resentments.

With this in mind, he announced his intention of putting into an Irish or French port to replace the inroads made already into the double consignments of wine and brandy. Irish captain of marines Will Betagh later claimed to have heard him swear several times that he would never join Clipperton again, but would proceed on his own. On his return to European waters from a successful voyage, he would avoid England and go on to Hamburg or some other free port and remain there, holding the owners to ransom for their cargo. If they went to law, he would use their own riches to fight them.

Some of the officers began to see all of the captain's recent actions as means to that end: his attempt to convince them that the *Success* had sunk in the storm, the reluctance to head south and look for the other ship. While they were still in port he had drunk the health of the owners many times, but as soon as they had put to sea, these demonstrations of loyalty had been replaced, Betagh testified, by his swearing, "Damn them! For my part I shall take care of Number One!"[3]

On that occasion Betagh had, apparently, waited for Second Capt. Simon "Sim" Hatley to speak up in the owners' defense, but he had remained silent. Hatley was an old shipmate of Clipperton's, having been third mate in Woodes Rogers's *Duchess*, and was thus very suspect in Shelvocke's mind.

So Betagh himself said to Shelvocke, "Sir, if I may have leave to offer my thoughts upon these frank declarations of your designs, it is my humble opinion that to act separately from Captain Clipperton will terminate in the ruin of this expedition."[4]

Testily Shelvocke replied, "No, no, we have a good ship, well-manned and sound, with all necessities. We shall do well enough."[5]

Stubbornly the Irishman went on, "Surely our owners would

have hardly put themselves to the expense of *two* ships, could they have had any reasonable prospect of making a good voyage with *one* in these remote parts?"[6]

Shelvocke shouted, "You are insolent, sir! Do you mean to usurp command of the ship?"[7]

Next day at dinner, Betagh pointedly toasted the owners, "to whom we are all indebted for this chance of making our fortunes."[8]

As he began to drink, Shelvocke flung his tankard at his head. "Sir, you insult my authority! You can be sure that the precious owners will be cunning enough on our return to defraud us of our proper dividends!"[9] Shelvocke may well have been thinking of the shabby treatment accorded Will Dampier after his last voyage. Both Betagh and Hatley agreed with Shelvocke that the ship was heavily pestered aloft, but they did not think her as "crank and tender" as the captain made out.

Hatley, generally thought to be a company man, had kept his own inscrutable councils until now. But a dispute with Shelvocke over a point of seamanship flamed into a quarrel. Shelvocke accused him also of trying to usurp his authority. The handsome second captain, speaking with his usual condescending sneer, stuck to his opinion. Shelvocke shouted furiously, "You see, gentlemen, how the villain disputes the command with me?"[10]

The quarrel broke out again later, in front of many of the ship's company, with Hatley claiming private orders from Hughes and Clipperton to take over the ship if he thought it necessary. "But do you have a private commission?" asked Shelvocke.[11]

Hatley sneered. "It is only just that I take over command, as I am the only man aboard this ship who has any knowledge of the South Seas!"[12]

But, unfortunately in terms of any authorization he might have had to this effect, Hatley had shown fear and incompetence during the storm and had lost the respect of the ship's company.

Shelvocke, however, realized that he would have to be careful, in future, not to provide another excuse for mutiny. He must humor his dissenters and work more subtly to get what he wanted out of this voyage.

Shelvocke had buttressed his personal interests, to some extent, with a few of his own appointees, including his nephew, surgeon Adams, and, of course, George Junior, whom the men called, contemptuously, Georgy. In their eyes he had no business on board, as his name was not among those subscribing to the ship's articles. According to Betagh, "He knew nothing of sea affairs or indeed of anything else that was commendable or manly. . . . His employment at London was to dangle after the women, and gossip at the tea table," and he "was more fit for a boarding school than a ship of war."[13] Georgy was also thought to be his father's spy.

Another of the captain's nominees was Matthew Stewart, his young great cabin steward. Stewart had at one time been supercargo in a small ship, but he was otherwise, according to Betagh, "not seaman enough to distinguish between a brace and a bowline," though a man of "good sense and good education," possibly on the run from the law—and, thus, a suitable assistant in any covert designs.[14] The men generally dismissed Stewart as Shelvocke's "winger" or "bum-boy."

Meanwhile, Shelvocke had thought better of his plan to put into an Irish or French port for more wine and brandy, which might well have revived the men's idea of returning home. He now altered course and headed for his first scheduled rendezvous with Clipperton, in the Canary Islands.

It was a tedious, often rough, passage for everyone. On the way Shelvocke perfunctorily hailed some of the ships encountered, but none had seen Clipperton and the *Success.* The *Speedwell* arrived in the Canaries on 17 March and cruised among the islands, ostensibly looking for Clipperton.

On the twenty-third, she overtook a small fisherman's barque of eighty or a hundred tons, and Shelvocke sent the launch after her. In the chase, the trawler ran aground. The launch's crew found nothing in her but some salt and a quarter-cask of wine, which the Britishers drank. All of his officers thought that Shelvocke should return the smack to her owner to pursue a living that was hard enough at the best of times, and concentrate on catching up with the *Success.* Clipperton's and Shelvocke's instructions had been to spend no more than ten days in the Canaries looking for each other, if they had become parted by then. Shelvocke now spent twelve days fitting the prize out with guns and sending her off to go through the motions of searching for Clipperton, whom, Shelvocke opined, must be long since gone.

There was no trace of the *Success* in the islands. The *Speedwell* sailed from Ferro (Hierro) on 29 March for the next rendezvous, which Shelvocke kept secret from his officers (off Cape St. Vincent in the Cape Verde Islands), taking her prize with her.

Morale on board continued low, with the crew restless and bloody-minded. While the officers were drinking together one evening, the gunner, Turner Stevens, made the serious proposal that they abandon the voyage and cruise in the Red Sea, where there should be rich pickings. There would be no harm, he said, in robbing "those Mahometans," whereas "the poor Spaniards" were "good Christians, and it would be sinful to injure them."[15] The dangerous brew of wine and brandy, called "hipsy," which was Shelvocke's favorite tipple, had got to the gunner's addled brain. Shelvocke had him confined belowdecks, from where he continually threatened to blow up the ship.

His example fired up the malcontents among the crew once more, and, as a precaution, Shelvocke had all the arms stowed away in the bread room under lock and key. The chief mate, Andrew

Pedder, was also a troublemaker, and several times he disputed Shelvocke's authority.

At six in the evening on 1 April, the *Speedwell* sighted the island of St. Vincent. There was no *Success* in view. After a token pause at the island, Shelvocke sailed southeast for the Isla of May (Maio) in the Portuguese Cape Verdes. Arriving there on 14 April in the forenoon, they saw a wreck. In spite of some wishful thinking on the *Speedwell*'s quarterdeck, it was not the *Success*, but Captain Hide's East Indiaman *Vanzittern*, which had run ashore three weeks earlier.

Shelvocke hoped for some planks and nails from the wreck, but other ships in the roadstead had been there before him. As the *Speedwell* approached the entrance to the roadstead, all nineteen ships of a convoy inside opened fire on her, thinking she was a freebooter. When Shelvocke had established his identity, the drunken commodore of the convoy and all of his masters came aboard to ask his pardon. They grandly promised him all he might need, though all he got, in the end, were a few sheeting boards and three and a half tons of salt. On the night after they anchored, the mutinous gunner and Chief Mate Pedder quarreled with First Lieutenant Brookes and attacked him. Shelvocke put them both ashore.

Before sailing again, Shelvocke took the dubious step of appointing his cabin steward, Matthew Stewart, chief mate. This caused more discontent among the ship's company, as Stewart was professionally unqualified for the job. At six in the morning on Wednesday 18 April, the *Speedwell* weighed from the Isla of May, and, in the same forenoon, arrived in the roadstead of Porto Praya, St. Jago Island (Sao Tiago).

The captain-major ashore here offered his help but produced only a small amount of fresh provisions. Shelvocke sold the *Speedwell*'s prize to the governor for 150 dollars. While the ship filled her water casks and was given a good heel, Shelvocke sent his kinsman, surgeon Adams, ashore to find out surreptitiously all he could about the movements of the *Success,* and to buy sugar for hipsy. Adams reported to him that Clipperton was said to have been at St. Vincent, news that Shelvocke kept from the rest of his officers.

On one trip ashore with the launch, four seamen—Henry Chapman, Cornelius Colson, William Parsons, and Christopher Terry—deserted. The governor refused to search for them, and Shelvocke dared not risk sending any more of his own discontented men on a search. He ordered the captain of a Portuguese ship to send a party ashore to apprehend them—or hand over the same number of his own men. The Portuguese recovered Chapman and Parsons for him, who, luckily, were the most valuable of the deserters, both good seamen and drummers. Once aboard, they fell on their knees and begged Shelvocke's pardon, accusing the captain-general of offering them bribes to join his service. Shelvocke was lenient and gained two faithful supporters, an endangered species.

The governor was wary of Shelvocke's honesty, and he swore again and again that there was nothing of value in the islands. Shelvocke was in no hurry to leave, particularly as both *Speedwell* and her rabble of a crew were in poor condition to weather Cape Horn. In particular, the ship's stern, with its wide-windowed lights, was vulnerable to a pooping sea. These doubts he kept to himself, rather than lower morale any further.

Besides his copy of Woodes Rogers's volume, Shelvocke had aboard A. F. Frezier's *Voyage to the South Sea and Along the Coasts of Chili and Peru,* which strongly recommended to any mariner intending to round the Horn that he refresh and repair at the island of St. Catherine, off the coast of Brazil, before hazarding the attempt.

It took *Speedwell* nearly two months of bad weather to reach Santa Caterina. On 4 June they sighted Cape Frio, Brazil, and, on the following afternoon, a ship was sighted flying the Portuguese flag.

Shelvocke steered for the Portuguese and sent an armed Sim Hatley in the five-oared boat to gather the latest news from the coast, with money to buy tobacco.

The Portuguese thought they were being boarded by pirates. As soon as Hatley reached their quarterdeck, before he had a chance to speak, they were handing down into *Speedwell*'s boat plantains, bananas, lemons, oranges, pomegranates, four dozen boxes of marmalade and other sweetmeats, Dutch cheeses, and quantities of sugar. To the Portuguese crew's huge relief, the "pirates" seemed satisfied with these gifts and shoved off again. Hatley did not show Shelvocke a purse bulging with moidores, which the Portuguese captain Don Pedro had handed over. On the return trip to the *Speedwell,* he bribed the coxswain with ten moidores and each oarsman with six of the heavy coins to keep quiet about it.

He did declare a dozen lengths of silk, some of it flowered with gold and silver, "worth at least three pound a yard," Hatley said, and several dozen china plates and bowls and a small Japanese lacquered cabinet.

When Shelvocke saw the spoils that the boat's crew dumped on the deck before him, he said to Hatley, "What do you mean by all this, sir?"

"By all what, sir?"

"Bringing me these baubles, sir."

"They are very cheap, sir."

"But I shall want my money for other uses. . . ."

"They'll fetch double the cost at our next port."

"You always act contrary to my orders!" shouted Shelvocke.

"Sir!" said Hatley indignantly, "I laid out my own money on the same things as yours!"

"It's a hard case I have no officer worth trusting," grumbled Shelvocke. "I can have nothing well done except I go out of the ship myself upon every occasion."

"I thought I had done for the better," sulked the second captain.

"I'll have you know, sir," said Shelvocke, "I'll be obeyed!"

"Your command shall always be to me as the law," sneered Hatley.

"Where is the account or bill of parcels?" demanded Shelvocke.

"Sir, not easily understanding one another, we lumped it, but I can draw one out."

"Pray see that you do."

"Yes, sir."

Shelvocke looked across the water at the Portuguese.

"Whither is he bound?"

"To Pernambuco."

"Where belonging to?"

"To Rio de Janeiro, whence he brought these fruits and refreshments which he presents you with, desiring me to give you his humble service, and that anything in his ship is at your disposal."

"Well, I believe he's a very honest fellow. Take the trumpet, tell him I thank him, and that he may pursue his voyage."

Hartley shouted, "Oh Señor Capitan, O ho!"

"Hola, Señor!" returned Don Pedro.

"Amigo, profiga u, m, fu camino con Dios."

Don Pedro muttered something. Hatley thought he caught something like "Y, u, m, el voestro con mille demonios, perro ladron."

"What does he say?" queried Shelvocke.

"'Go, you thieving dog, and a thousand devils along with you,'" said Hatley, "or some such thing." Don Pedro hoisted his topsails and made haste to be off.[16]

A few days later all the *Speedwell*'s petty officers and boats' crews appeared in fine silk waistcoats, caps and breeches, seaman officers in scarlet suits, marines in green, Shelvocke in a black silk suit trimmed with large silver loops down the chest. He called it his "peau de soy," or "silk skin."

Next day they sighted a ship, which the men wanted to hail, but Shelvocke forbade it. If she was the *Success* he did not want to know it. He would carry on alone.

At last, in the forenoon of 19 June, after fifty-five days of rough weather, it was "Land ho!" from the masthead. The ship anchored safely in six fathoms.

3

Levellers' Talk

St. Catherine's Island, some 8.5 leagues (twenty-five miles) by 2 leagues (six miles), was almost completely covered by thick woods and brambles, broken only by Portuguese plantations offering oranges, lemons, limes, bananas, melons, cabbages, potatoes, and some very expensive rum made from poorly cultivated sugarcane. There was hardly any game, though the woods were loud with parrots that made very good eating, and exotic macaws, cockatoos, and pink flamingos.

The sea was full of fish. Bays and creeks bulged with mullet, large rays, grunters, "cavillies" (horse mackerel), and "drum fish," so called because of the agitated noise they made. This made it easy to follow them into shoal water; some weighed twenty to thirty pounds. There were delicious small green oysters on rocks and stones and mangrove roots, "sea-eggs," sea green or deep purple, containing yellowish meat that "exceeds all the shell-fish I ever tasted,"[1] Shelvocke noted. Huge prawns were netted. Cattle grazed the fertile land, and the air was sweet.

The numerous black cattle had been brought from the great herds that grazed the savannas of the mainland. Settlers enjoyed the blessings of the fertile country and wholesome air. They had very few needs, even for clothes. The only guns they kept were for use against jaguars, which Shelvocke called tigers, and each house kept a pack of dogs, even though one jaguar had been known to kill as many as eight or ten of them. The big cats' prints on the sandy shore were very common. There was no evidence of the fine dwelling houses mentioned by Frezier, no towns or villages. There were only some fortified places in the woods, making good retreats from enemies, which soon included the men of the *Speedwell.* St. Catherine's was a demi-paradise that the rapacious tars of the ship's polyglot crew did their best to spoil, serpents in a Garden of Eden.

Emanuel Mansa, the captain-general of St. Catherine's, and, at first, many of the islanders visited the ship daily. They brought fresh provisions. Some of these were bartered for salt, of which the natives were, as reported by Frezier, always short. The large gift of salt from the Isla of May convoy came in handy. Shelvocke bought, according to his final report, 60 cheese, 300 pounds of butter, and 21 head of black cattle, but Betagh chronicled only 4 head. Likewise, Shelvocke says he indented for 150 bushels of caffader meal. Betagh saw only 6 come aboard, and he claimed that none of the other provisions listed by Shelvocke ever reached the hold or galley, except for 5 hogs.

Shelvocke decided to sit out the southern winter in this happy isle. He was in no hurry to face the Horn—or to find Clipperton.

Then, somehow, the locals picked up the buzz flying along the coast that the British ship had robbed the Portuguese ship off Cape Frio. They refused any further trade with Shelvocke and burned down the house where *Speedwell*'s coopers and sailmakers worked. It took an impassioned appeal by La Porte, the ship's second lieutenant, who was a Frenchman and a Roman Catholic, to the island's priest, to reinstate the provisioning of the *Speedwell,* but relations between settlers and sailors remained bad.

On 2 July 1719, the morning watch reported a large ship lying at anchor off Parrott's Island, about five miles below where *Speedwell* lay. Alarmed, Shelvocke first satisfied himself that she was not the *Success,* and he sent Lt. Sam Randall off in the launch, well-manned and armed, to check her identity. Randall had strict orders not to go on board her for any reason whatever. Shelvocke mounted guns at the watering places and singled up to the anchor, ready for a quick defense.

By noon, Shelvocke had just about given up his boat for lost when she returned. A well-oiled Randall told him that the stranger was the *Ruby,* a former British man-of-war, now French and commanded by Capitaine La Jonquière. The ship had been in Spanish service in the South Sea but had sailed for home when news of war between Spain and France had reached her.

Shelvocke was suspicious of this story, and he reprimanded Randall for his disobedience. The befuddled lieutenant, who was First Lieutenant Brookes's brother-in-law, professed to have been talked into it. Shelvocke pointed out that had the *Ruby* been an enemy, he would now be short one lieutenant and, far worse, twenty-three good men.

Next day *Ruby* up-anchored and made toward them. Shelvocke manned his guns. La Jonquière anchored short of him and sent across a lieutenant and a priest to assure the Englishman of his friendship and invite him to dinner.

The *Ruby* carried a rich treasure in gold and silver, as well as a large number of wealthy passengers. If Shelvocke was tempted, he thought better of it. *Ruby* had fifty-four guns mounted.

La Jonquière told him that the Spanish in the South Sea knew of the English privateers and their mission, and that they were fitting out men-of-war to give them a hot reception. Shelvocke begged him to keep this to himself. If his rabble of a crew heard of it, they would probably refuse to go any farther.

Some time later, when La Jonquière and his officers were dining aboard *Speedwell,* there was a loud fracas outside the great cabin. Shelvocke found Hudson, the bosun, already smoldering with the grudge that his position on board did not receive the respect it deserved. He protested at not being invited to dine, when "lesser men than I, who should be regarded as the third man in the ship, are gathered to indulge their unearned privileges." Betagh and Adams then appeared. "Bloodsuckers!" shouted Hudson, and he attacked them, but *Speedwell* and *Ruby* officers subdued him.[2]

On 15 July a big ship entered the harbor mouth, saw the English and French ships, and made a hasty retreat out again. La Jonquière, who had been in the service of Spain, now his country's enemy, was nervous about strange ships that might be out to punish him. At nightfall he weighed and slipped down the harbor, putting out to sea at first light and saluting the *Speedwell* with five guns. With him went bosun Hudson and three Frenchmen from *Speedwell*'s crew, which received in exchange a surly Irishman named Will Morphew, who turned out to be a bad bargain but made himself useful as the ship's cobbler.

The ship's carpenter was proceeding very slowly with the woodcutting, blaming blunt axes and saws and unskilled men. There were no nails for boarding up the stern, "Chippy" (the carpenter) having sold most of his stores before the ship had reached Plymouth. The armorer made some nails with the help of a forge and bellows, given to the ship by La Jonquière, but that took time.

Then, on 25 July, the ship that had poked her nose into the harbor came back in, flying French colors. She was the *Sage Solomon* of St. Malo, forty guns, commanded by Capitaine Gérard Dumain, bound for Chile and Peru to trade. Shelvocke bought some very expensive nails from him, and Dumain abused La Jonquière as a renegade for serving under a foreign flag.

The cooper's men made new casks and filled them with fresh water. Meat casks were broached, and the contents repickled. Rigging and sails were overhauled. Most of the guns were stowed in the hold to lower the ship's center of gravity and make the top-heavy *Speedwell* less given to extreme angles of roll. Just as Shelvocke thought he was about ready to leave for the Horn, the newly promoted chief mate, Matt Stewart, came to the great cabin with a letter from the crew. It was a threat: if the demands it contained were not met to the full, they would not "stir a step to sea."

"Honoured sir," ran the letter, "we have very good reason to believe that if what we have the fortune to make on this voyage should be carried to London, we should never receive half thereof; for it is known to all how the people on board the ships *Duke* and *Duchess* [Woodes Rogers's ships] were treated, and if we carry our money to London, can expect no better treatment." Dampier had died in 1715, his share as pilot of the *Duke* still unpaid. "How dangerous is it for poor men to trust their fortune in the hands of rich men?" The letter went on:

> By sharing the money as soon as possible, we design nothing against the good of the voyage and Owners, for we shall do all our endeavours to see them get their shares, and as to our desiring plunder, we have desired nothing but what the people on board the Duke and Duchess had before us. We hope you will not take it amiss that we have made bold to present you with what we will insist upon as our due right, which is designed for no harm to the owners, and to the good of us all; we are sure it will make everything to be easy among us, and it will always make us willing to venture our lives in behalf of ourselves and owners. You may also be assured of our respect towards you. We shall always think ourselves happy under such a commander.

It was signed "with all humble respect" by mates Matthew Stewart, James Hopkins, and John Sprake; carpenter Robert Davenport; gunner Gilbert Henderson; ensign of marines Gilbert Hamilton; Nicholas Laming; and surgeon's mates William Morgan and John Doidge. Besides these, all the petty officers and thirty-six of the chief foremast-men put their signatures or made their marks on the letter. It was reasonably literate and the tone tactful but firm, the work of a semi-educated man. Shelvocke recognized Matt Stewart's hand and realized that he had been nurturing and favoring that worst of all cuckoos in the crow's nest, a sea lawyer.

On the back of the letter were the "Articles" drawn up by the men for the regulation of plunder:

> Inprimis, That our part of each prize we take shall be equally divided, as soon as possible, after the capture thereof, between the ship's company, according to each man's respective shares, as borne on the ship's books.
>
> Secondly, That all plunder on board each prize we take shall be equally divided among the ship's company. . . .
>
> Thirdly, That gold rings found in any place, except in a goldsmith's shop, is plunder, all arms, sea books and instruments, all clothing and moveables usually worn about prisoners (except women's ear-rings, unwrought gold and silver, loose diamonds, pearls and money), all plate in use aboard ships, but not on shore (unless about the persons of prisoners) is plunder; all manner of clothes ready-made, found on the upper deck or between decks, belonging to the ship's company and passengers, is plunder also, except what is above limited, and is in bundles of pieces, that appears not for the person's use . . . but designed for merchandise, which only shall not be plunder; all manner of bedding, all manner of necessaries, all buttons, buckles, liquors and provisions, for our expending and use, is plunder. . . .
>
> Fourthly, That if any person on board the ship do conceal any plunder, exceeding one piece of eight, twenty-four hours after the capture of the prize, he shall be severely punished, and lose his share of that prize and plunder, one half thereof to be given to the informer, and the other to be divided among the ship's company. . . .
>
> Fifthly, That all plunder shall be appraised and divided as soon as possible after the capture; also every person to be sworn and searched as soon as they come aboard. The person refusing shall forfeit their share of prize or plunder as above.
>
> Sixthly, In consideration that Captain Shelvocke, to make the ship's company easy, will give up the whole cabin plunder (which

> in all probability is the major part) to be divided as aforesaid, we do voluntarily agree that he shall have five per cent over and above his respective share, as a consideration of what is his due of the plunder aforesaid.
>
> Seventhly, That a reward of twenty dollars shall be given to him that first sees a prize of good value, or exceeding fifty tons in burthen.[3]

Shelvocke showed the document to his officers. It reminded some of the older ones of the Levellers' revolutionary doctrine. The old marine lieutenant was about the only man on board old enough to remember the once politically active and influential democratic party known as the Levellers, because of their apparent aim to "level men's estates." Their movement had begun in the civil war among Puritan soldiers of Oliver Cromwell's Model Army, to whom were owed considerable arrears of pay. They formed revolutionary councils and declared for the formation of a republic in England. They gained massive support when the Independent Party in Parliament split into moderates and Leveller sympathizers. The latter spoke of revolution, votes for all, and the restriction by force of property owning to those with "natural right"—gained only by personal effort. "The poorest he that is in England hath a right to live as well as the greatest he," declared Leveller leader Rainsborough.[4]

The Levellers were fiercely opposed by the Presbyterians in Parliament (the Tories of those turbulent years after the civil war), and by the Monarchists. Levellers in the still-powerful Cromwellian army formed revolutionary councils to make all decisions. Cromwell himself called the Levellers, whose conspiracy had found strong support even in the regiment he himself had raised, "little better than beasts."

At the other extreme were the Royalists, who formed armed assemblies and kidnapped assize judges. Both parties were declared illegal, and leading "Cavaliers" and Levellers alike filled the prisons, including the democratic member of Parliament Lilburne, a tireless pamphleteer in the latter cause. The lesser conspirators were transported to work on West Indian plantations.

Unlike the army, the navy remained largely uninfluenced by socialistic doctrine. Thanks originally to King Charles I's unpopular "ship money" levies, it had grown into an able, professional standing force, especially under the Commonwealth's Admiral Blake, who instilled pride into the sailors by resounding victories over royal exiles and the Dutch. Conditions of pay and provisioning had, in general, also greatly improved, and there was little discontent upon which agitators could play.

After the restoration of the monarchy in 1660, however, with the appointment of incompetent, arrogant, often debauched Cavaliers as navy officers and even captains of major warships, the situation changed. There was "Levellers' talk" 'tween decks, and it persisted and flourished wherever there was neglect, ill-treatment, or delays over pay in any of His Majesty's ships.

Some of the *Speedwell*'s hands, previously pressed against their will into naval service, had Leveller connections in their families or had picked up dissension in prison, and they spread insubordination. Some restless elements in the fo'c'sle had found a leader in Chief Mate Stewart. Shelvocke's former protégé was the son of a man who had shouted revolution at the great Levellers' meeting at Putney Church in London, in October 1647. He himself wanted to create in one of His Majesty's ships a revolutionary council along the old Roundhead army Leveller lines. The St. Catherine's agreement was only the beginning.

Shelvocke's own public slandering of the owners had given him some encouragement. After Shelvocke had read the document, Stewart said he was simply a messenger, sent by his shipmates to receive an answer. And, he confided, it had better, in his opinion, be favorable to them, as they were determined to get their share of whatever treasure might fall to the *Speedwell* before it passed into the owners' hands—though they would always do justice to the latter.

Stewart's tone was that of a faithful servant forced to convey threats that were distasteful to himself—a hypocritical stance often adopted in later years by trade-union officials. Shelvocke had noticed that the envy and suspicion originally accorded the unfairly promoted chief mate seemed to have changed to a more cordial acceptance. He now knew why, though he saw the influence of Second Captain Hatley in the inside knowledge of the treatment of Woodes Rogers's men. Hatley had been an officer in the *Duchess,* whose men had not only received less than one-tenth of their due from the plunder taken, but had also been cheated of their joining-ship pay. This also explained how the second captain came to be such a favorite with "the people," all at once, in contrast with their attitude toward him after his poor showing during the early gales.

Shelvocke said piously that he could not be a party to anything prejudicial to the owners, to whom he had sworn faithfully to follow instructions, without losing both his reputation and his fortune. He asked the men to wait until they met the *Success* in the Pacific and put the matter before Commodore Clipperton, if they had even a tenth of the respect they professed for him. But on consulting his officers, he found that many of them tacitly agreed with the proposals, and Hatley said that if he knew Clipperton, the commodore would approve of them too.

There followed a few days of uneasy consultation on both sides, with dark mutterings from the crew and no work being done. Then the hands gathered on the quarterdeck in a threatening mood, demanding to know the captain's response to their terms, which they swore to stand by, whatever the outcome, as the best way they knew of providing for themselves against shadowy rewards for the uncertain risks facing them.

To give the affair a semblance of legal respectability, Stewart came forward with "A copy of the Power of Attorney and Agency made to Matthew Stewart by the ship's company on board the *Speedwell.*" It read:

> Know all men by these presents, that we undersubscribers, officers, seamen and others, on board the *Speedwell* of London, Captain George Shelvocke commander, for certain good causes us hereunto moving, have and do hereby name our trusty friend Matthew Stewart our true and lawful attorney and agent, to recover all and singular such wages, salaries, prize-money, etc., whatsoever, as now is or shall be due, payable and belonging to us for our service on board the ship *Speedwell,* or any prize or prizes taken by her.[5]

Seeing their determination, with the prospect of meeting Clipperton in the South Sea uncertain, and believing that his refusal to sign the articles could mean the men taking over the ship—if not worse, for himself and his few supporters—Shelvocke signed the agreement. All the officers then followed his example, some with private reservations. Betagh saw a Machiavellian touch by the captain himself in the whole affair, even to the extent of suggesting that the ex-purser had instigated the "mutiny" himself, through the agency of Stewart and/or Hatley, as he stood to gain in fortune by it, if not in reputation.

Shelvocke had recognized in the fo'c'sle document a reflection of his own, and most seafarers', mistrust of owners. Many were the honest seamen in mercantile service who had been cheated, by downright fraud or by bureaucratic procrastination ashore, of their share of prize money and pay. Once ashore, with all dangers past, all risks run, all hardships overcome, all glory gained, they had no voice, no vote, no representation. The families of the living could live on a crust, those of the dead could starve. The owners grew fat.

Ostensibly, the St. Catherine's document was this voice, a cry for justice and fair dealing. It was not mutiny, except in the threat to withdraw labor. The owners were promised their half-share of all profit. The Speedwells, at least the honest tars among them, simply wanted the only sure guarantee of their share—by fait accompli, by holding it in their hands.

How, practically, this was to be done was not addressed in the document. Division of material spoils at the capstan head was obviously impossible, fraught as that was with the threat of division and violence. The only means of fair allotment, first between owners' and crews' shares, then among the men, was by the conversion of assets, prizes, or plunder into cash or scrip, with hard, hot coin the seaman's preferred portion. Even if the plan could be fairly administered, there were many among this ragtag crew who would use it as a robbers' charter. By signing it Shelvocke could be opening the door to outright piracy.

The signing seemed to strengthen Shelvocke in his stand against what he saw as disloyalty among his officers. His first act was to gather them all together in his great cabin and peremptorily appoint surgeon Adams, his nephew, as agent to represent their interests against the men. Stunned by events, they offered no opposition, only a murmur of dissent from Betagh. There was a shocked protest, however, from owners' agent Hendry when Shelvocke proposed to take his place, offering him the post of purser in lieu. As owners' agent, Hendry could claim a 20 percent share of their profits, as purser only what Shelvocke chose to give him. He demanded his right to a council of officers to judge the matter. Shelvocke refused. Hendry drew up a protest, which he circulated among the officers.

But Shelvocke had not finished his reassignments. He now proposed to reduce Betagh to a lieutenant of marines, the two lieutenants to petty officers. The Irishman took out his pocketbook and handed Shelvocke a letter from Edward Hughes, authorizing his appointment. Shelvocke said no more on the matter, but two days later the pocketbook, containing, besides Hughes's letter, some memoranda on Shelvocke's conduct, was stolen from Betagh's cabin.

Betagh continued to make notes on Shelvocke's behavior. It was clearly the captain's duty, he thought, to press south around the Horn. He should get to grips with the Spaniards as soon as possible, to forestall any special measures the latter might take if Clipperton had already tipped them off to the presence of English privateers. He should join Clipperton, to present as powerful a combined force as possible. "But our commander found it more comfortable," wrote Betagh, "to pass the winter away near that glorious luminary the sun, than at the hazard of losing his liquors to follow his orders and his commodore into that frozen Strait of Magellan."[6]

A Spanish Creole, servant to one of La Jonquière's lieutenants, had robbed his master of 400 quadruples (about 1,600 pistoles, or 1,444 pounds) and fled to the woods on the island, intending to join the *Speedwell* and round the Horn, back to his own country again. La Jonquière had asked Shelvocke to put the man in irons if he showed up, and, if he had the stolen money on him, to remit it to them in France when the *Speedwell* reached home. Shelvocke had promised to do so. As soon as the *Ruby* sailed, the thief turned up at the watering place with one moiety of the money in his pocket to pay for his passage. Shelvocke took the money and had the man seized up to the jeers, where he was flogged. This was repeated every Monday for a month, but the man did not reveal the whereabouts of any more of the money.

"Thus was Shelvocke," wrote Betagh, "with his wholesome severities, teaching the Spaniard the heinousness of defrauding his master, when we all very well knew Shelvocke deserved the same disipline himself."[7]

Before the *Speedwell* sailed from St. Catherine's a French merchantman came in from St. Malo, commanded by Capitaine Dumain Girard, bound for Chile. The ship had met the *Ruby* at sea, and La Jonquière had requested that Girard secure any recovered money from Shelvocke. But Shelvocke insisted on sticking to the original arrangement, and kept what he had taken off the thief.

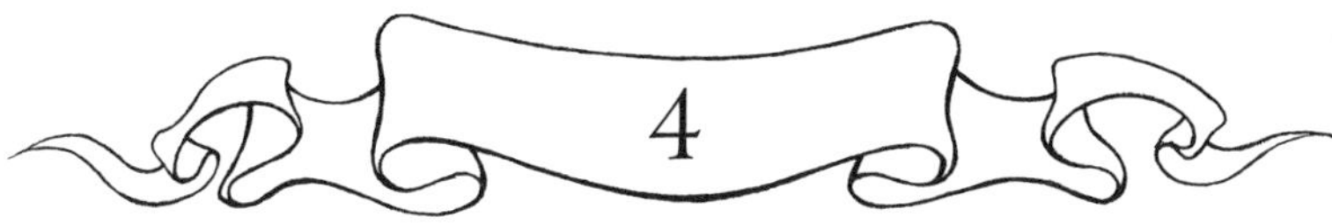

4 The Albatross

On 3 August 1719, a Portuguese man-of-war, the *St. Francis Xavier,* forty guns, commanded by Capitaine La Rivière, another Frenchman, came in from Lisbon. Ostensibly she was bound for Macao, China, but Shelvocke, certain that her captain must have heard of the Cape Frio incident, wondered if he had orders to deal with the English privateer. Shelvocke ordered Hatley to convey his compliments to the French captain, and to "vindicate yourself to try to forestall any unpleasantness."

Hatley returned and told Shelvocke that La Rivière had not spoken of the matter at all. But Shelvocke was not reassured, and he determined to leave the island as soon as possible. He sent men to track down three deserters, but the Portuguese were now thoroughly disgusted with the *Speedwell*'s gang of thieves and bullies, and an armed mob drove them back to the boat, shouting, "Kill the dogs! Kill all the English dogs!" and fired a volley at the retreating jack-tars, wounding three of them. Hatley, who had been carrying on an affair with the wife of the captain-general, was attacked by him with shouts of, "This is the villain! This is the man who called me cuckold!"[1] The handsome second captain was lucky to get away.

On 9 August *Speedwell* weighed for the Horn, cattle and hogs crowding the decks, stores full of salted fish; cassava flour, which made a good instant burgoo (porridge); a stock of tobacco; and calavance beans.

Steering south, never more than twenty to thirty leagues from the South American mainland, the "Desert Coast," the ship hit squally weather, with Second Lieutenant La Porte breaking a leg in a fall on deck. They sighted seals and penguins, pintado birds, their black and white feathers arranged like a checkerboard, and solitary albatrosses, "the largest of sea fowls," as Shelvocke called them in his log. As the mouth of the River Plate opened out, the sea became covered with huge rafts of seaweed, which often slowed or stopped the blunt-bowed *Speedwell,* clinging to her stubbornly.

"Englishmen," wrote Samuel Pepys, "and more especially seamen, love their bellies above everything else, and therefore it must always be remembered, in the management of the victualling of the Navy, that to make any abatement from them in the quantity or agreeableness of the victuals is to discourage and provoke them in the tenderest point."[2]

As they advanced south, Shelvocke recorded, "My people's stomachs increased, to that degree that the allowance which the Government gives in the Navy is not sufficient to satisfy their hunger. Some of my officers in particular were very angry that they could not have their bellies full or at least a greater share than the common people."[3]

Will Betagh was the most vociferous. Shelvocke often accused him of taking more than his fair share. But Betagh maintained that the captain's lack of interest in food, in preference to a liquid lunch, probably made his own consumption look excessive. Shelvocke felt compelled to divide the food on the officers' table into equal parts to ensure fair shares.

Shelvocke also accused Betagh of inciting the men to demand extra rations. Eventually he was forced to give the hands an extraordinary meal every day, of porridge or calavances. This made serious inroads into their wood and water.

In a furious row with Shelvocke, Betagh said, "I hope in God this voyage will be short with you!" This convinced Shelvocke that the Irishman intended to take over the ship, aided by Hatley, Brookes and his incompetent brother-in-law Sam Randall, sea lawyer Stewart, and the other Irish malcontent, Morphew.

He confined Betagh to the steerage. Food was brought down to him, and when he wanted to relieve himself, a sentry with drawn sword accompanied him. He was confined like this for fourteen days, with no one daring to speak to him. Then he sent Shelvocke a note full of regret for giving him "such language as is in no way justifiable from any officer to his commander," and Shelvocke released him.[4]

By 19 September, Shelvocke was looking for the shoal that was said by Frezier to lie close off the mouth of the Straits of Magellan. He stood in for the land once, but could do no better with the lead than fifty-five fathoms. He turned along the coast again, finally coming up with the Straits of Magellan but passing them by, in favor of the more southernmost Straits of Le Maire, following Clipperton's dubious recommendation. Shelvocke the veteran navigator and canny seaman appreciated the danger of wearing out his "ground tackling" by the frequent sounding and anchoring likely to be demanded in the tortuous waterways of Magellan, not to mention the wear and tear on the men.

Fog bedeviled them, and the masthead lookouts swayed up there in a world of their own, above the murk. Then the fog cleared. There to starboard were mountains of a stupendous height on Tierra del Fuego, entirely covered with snow. It was a silent, barren landscape, some eight leagues distant. Then the mist returned, a sudden ghostly clamminess. Shelvocke brought to, and they began to feel the onset of the "Cape Horn sickness," which afflicts all mariners even today, about to attempt the dreaded passage.

By the end of the middle watch, they were making an easy sail to the southeast. At dawn, it was clear enough to make out that the *Speedwell* had made landfall about five leagues northwest of

North Sea

South Sea

Albemarle Isle

Cape Sebbanco

Cape S. Bartholomew: Lat 55:00 S.

The Straights of Lemaire 54:45 S.

Port of Good Success

Rocks of Montegordo

Isle of S. Gonzalo

Mount of S. Alifonto

Isle of Diego Ramiras

Terra del Fogua

Cape S. Yves

Cape of Rocks

Entry of S. Sebastian

Point of Arina

C. Holy Ghost

C. Virgin Mary

R. Gallegos

Jesus Bay

Bay of S. Phillip

Great Bay

S. Galentine

Hills of Lobes

Straights of Magellan

Kings Citty

Cape Victoria

4 Evangelists

C. Desire

12: Apostles

From the Port of S. Vizente (I mean the port of Carimapo near the Isle of Chilae) to the Straights of Magellan is 175 Leagues: this Straights lyes in the Lat. of 52:30 S. & from thence to the Straights of Lemaire is 75 Leagues N.W. & S.E.

The Straights of Magellan is in Length 110 Leagues and the Straights of Lemaire is but 8 Leagues from N. to S.

Southern entrances to the Pacific, from Hack's *Wagoner of the Great South Sea.*
(National Maritime Museum, England)

Capt. Bartholomew Sharpe had served under Henry Morgan in the first piratical attack on Panama in 1671. In 1679, he led a second attempt. This was abortive, but he sacked Porto Bello and Santa Maria, then cruised in a captured barque, taking prizes and holding towns to ransom. On 29 July 1681, he captured the *Rosario,* with a fortune in silver and a *derroterro,* or atlas, a large book of sea charts and maps of the South Sea and the coasts of Spanish America, together with sailing directions. Sharpe eventually returned home around the Horn. To mollify the Spanish ambassador, he was tried for piracy.

His acquittal may have been for want of hard evidence, in tacit approval of his activities, or it may have been a result of the impact made by his most important booty, the *derroterro* from the *Rosario.* Sharpe took the atlas and his own journal of the voyage to William Hack of Wapping, near London. Hack had himself been a buccaneer in his youth, but now flourished as a transcriber of notable voyages and a copier of maps. He had the Spanish sailing directions translated by one Philip Dassigny, and in 1685, he produced an English volume entitled *Wagoner of the Great South Sea,* which Sharpe presented to King Charles II. This contained the first reasonably accurate navigational charts of the Pacific to be seen in England.

King Charles appointed Sharpe a captain in the Navy, and he commanded the sloop *Bonetta.* He deserted his ship, however, captured a small Dutch vessel off Ramsgate, England, and sailed back to the West Indies. He was last heard of as leader of a band of pirates on the island of Anguilla.

Le Maire. This treacherous channel of wild water between the mainland and Staten Island was as intimidating to eighteenth-century mariners as were Scylla and Charybdis to the ancients, but Shelvocke proposed to face its hazards.

The passage to the westward later named Beagle Channel, between mainland Tierra del Fuego and its archipelago, was unexplored at the time, and Shelvocke was set on the Cape Horn passage. To ignore Le Maire and pass south around Staten Island would entail too much westering to round the Horn against fierce and almost constant contrary winds, exposing the crank and tender old vessel and her enfeebled crew to too great a strain.

First they were sucked into the Straits, then a northern tide drove them out again. When this tide shifted to windward, a short, sharp sea arose, so steep that the wildly pitching *Speedwell* dunked her bowsprit and stern lantern alternately. Bearing out her reputation for "rolling on wet meadow grass," she labored violently and would not answer her helm. Not until midnight did the cruel tide shift, and she got through the Straits, steering south, with the wind still brisk from the southwest, the land only a muzzy blur. In the morning, she had made a very good offing southward, before hauling round sou'westward.

Speedwell's anchors were unstocked and brought aft, and the spritsail yard got in to make everything as snug as possible. The cold that had begun to attack them grew rapidly worse, as their bows plunged on toward the Horn. The bleak westerly winds themselves would have been piercing enough, but they were attended by driving snow or sleet, which beat continuously on sails, decks, and rigging and coated the masts and every rope on the ship with ice, making the sails almost useless.

Although the Speedwells had got used to the most severe storms and thought it tolerable weather if they could bear a reefed mainsail—and it was common to lie for two or three days with bare poles, exposed to the battering of prodigious seas—they were now relying very much on the shelter of the awning that the sail-maker and his party had made at St. Catherine's. The tempestuous westerlies battered them without letup, and continuous fog brought the fear of hitting jagged ice flows, formed from the white cliffs of glaciers as they reached the sea. They seldom saw the sun, and sailing master Blowfield Coldsea managed only one observation in this whole passage to westward of Le Maire.

At seven one evening, when the hands were furling the mainsail, seaman Will Cammell cried out that his hands were so numb that he could not hold on. Before those next to him could come to his help, he fell into the icy sea, where it was a narrow line between being drowned or frozen to death almost instantaneously. Although they were now in the summer season in these parts, with very long days, they were hit continuously by sudden vicious squalls of sleet, snow, and rain that scoured the channels of Tierra del Fuego, with the sky perpetually hidden by foreboding clouds. It seemed impossible that any living thing could subsist in so rigid a climate, and they all realized that they had not seen fish of any kind since leaving the Straits of Le Maire, nor one seabird except, says Shelvocke, "a disconsolate black albatross who accompanied us as if he had lost himself."[5]

More than a dozen species of these great sea fliers cruised the Atlantic and Pacific Ocean altitudes, from the Aleutians to Antarctica. The Wandering Albatross, widest winged (up to twelve feet) of its kind and the most spectacular glider, was rivaled only by its land-based counterpart, the mighty condor, which sailed on the icy gusts howling through the mountains. Both birds could stay aloft for weeks, without ever flapping their very long, narrow-chord, maximum-lift wings, the albatross having spent from five to ten years at sea learning pelagic navigation and feeding techniques.

The Wanderer lived in the air, gliding on the constant blow of the Roaring Forties, and going ashore only to breed. The raging winds of the Horn that destroyed ships were its highroads. At night it perched on the surging waves to gobble squid, which surfaced at dusk. In the daytime it fed off schooling fish, exhausted or wounded birds, the carrion flesh of dead whales, and waste food from ships. It drank seawater.

It often attached itself to solitary ships in the Southern Ocean. With its spectacular performance and black wings, it had long been the pelagic sailor's closest familiar, and the superstitious mariner had attached various myths to it. Albatross were sometimes said to represent or contain the souls of dead sailors, and to be the bringers of good or bad luck. To kill one brought the inevitable wrath of Neptune. In spite of this, starving sailors caught them on baited hooks, and they were slaughtered for their feathers, used in millinery as "swansdown."

Judging by its wingspan and black outer wings, *Speedwell*'s albatross was a Wanderer or possibly a Royal Albatross, which was very similar but generally a little smaller. Shelvocke watched it appreciatively as it rode the storm so easily and gracefully, with only an occasional beat of its wide wings. The bird had easily overtaken the *Speedwell* and continued to circle her, flying upwind by diving to a low altitude above the sea, where the wind velocity was lower than a few yards higher up. "How clumsy and inept was our own display with sail, reef and rudder, in comparison!" recorded Shelvocke.[6]

Sim Hatley was less impressed. In one of his frequent bouts of deep depression, he remarked that the albatross might well be an ill omen, bringing bad luck. The series of contrary tempestuous winds that had oppressed them ever since the black bird had joined them seemed to support him. After some shots had fallen short, at length he hit and killed the albatross, when it swooped low to feed.

But its death brought no respite from the pounding of wind and sea. Far distant from any port to have recourse to in case of the loss of masts or any other accident, with no chance of receiving assistance from any other ship, now Shelvocke missed the *Success.* Morale sank as they all listened to the creaking of the masts, expecting them any moment to fall. The daydreams of a long repose in the Pacific Ocean on the bullion coast of Peru died amid the howling winds.

At eight o'clock one night, the *Speedwell* carried away her foretopmast. Shelvocke drove his wretched tars into rigging another next morning. They struggled up on the icy mast to secure it, with everyone mindful of Will Cammell's awful end. By slow degrees the ship crept onward toward the edge of the world. Shelvocke does not record a clear sighting of Cape Horn, but there came a time when the seas seemed to change in character, where the South Atlantic and the Pacific Oceans met. Then they rode the crests of waves that had originated eight thousand miles to the west, off the great, unexplored continent of Australia.

The grip of the contrary winds gradually lessened, though this was barely discernible to the exhausted, frozen yardsmen. The battered, boarded-up, top-heavy old vessel had withstood the worst weather. Her masts still groaned in the wind but did not topple. Bare yards keened in the gusts, but most of them stayed firm. At last, at noon on Saturday 14 November, they sighted the coast of Chile.

5

Capitaine le Breton

As they were now within the jurisdiction of the Spanish settlements in Chile, it was advisable to proceed with the greatest caution to avoid being recognized. However, the extra meal served had used up wood and water so greedily that it was important to stock up again. They had only seven butts of water left, and an even smaller proportion of firing wood. The water butts were stowed in such a way that it would mean unstowing half the hold to get at them.

A study of what charts he had and the relevant chapter of Frezier's book told Shelvocke that Narborough Island was probably their best bet for provisions. At eight in the morning on Thursday 19 November 1719, they sighted land. At noon, the greater mass of the island bore northeast, three leagues distant.

On Saturday 21 November, soundings taken at seven in the morning registered a depth of twenty-eight fathoms, with a bottom of fine gray and black sand. But the sea in the roadstead was very wild. At nine o'clock Shelvocke steered east-a-half north for the mouth of the Santo Domingo river, opposite the island on the Chilean mainland. At that point it appeared to be uninhabited, with an abundance of trees and cool, sparkling streams.

As the ship dipped her bows in the river, the depth decreased dramatically to four fathoms. Shelvocke hastily went about and headed out to sea again, not wanting to risk a grounding in this unfrequented place. The *Speedwell* ranged along the shore, trying several bays that looked very commodious but were all foul-bottomed.

Next day thick, wet weather blew them northward. Shelvocke professed to want to reach Juan Fernandez Island as quickly as possible without stopping anywhere. But the bare state of the *Speedwell*'s cupboard made it necessary to look for dry provisions as well as wood, and repairs were necessary to the crank and tender, and, by now, gale-battered ship, with the fierce sou'westerlies trying their best to wreck her on a lee shore.

A French seaman in the ship's company, Joseph de la Fontaine, assured Shelvocke that he would find everything he could want on the island of Chiloe, just to the northward. In fact, to hear him talk, there was no place like Chiloe in the South Sea. The soil of the island was very fertile, producing all kinds of European fruits and grains, with fine pasturing for big herds of sheep and cattle. The air was wholesome, the climate temperate, and there were plenty of tasty fowl and geese. A small woolen industry produced fine carpets and clothes. Boxes, chests, escritoires, and the like were expertly carved in the native cedar wood, and the whole of Chile and Peru were supplied with hams and tongues, and lumber. . . .

The Spaniards there always brutally crushed any sign of insurrection, but they were few, now, with rusty old weapons and crumbling fortifications. Chiloe could probably be taken easily. The Spaniards' chief security in the area, as in the whole of South America and Mexico, was the power of the Jesuits, who maintained a wealthy college on the mainland at Calibuco.

Spurred on by the French matelot's portrait of the earthly paradise, the men rushed to rope and tackle. Shelvocke reasoned that if they passed up this chance of replenishment, the crew might well demand to cross the South Sea in search of rich pickings in the Indian Ocean. After storing ship at Chiloe, they could hole up at some deserted island until the Spaniards thought they must have abandoned coastal waters, then make a sudden surprise sortie and fall upon enemy ships and treasuries.

Of course, they only had la Fontaine's word that Chiloe was a cornucopia. It was one of the largest of an archipelago of many islands, most of them uninhabited. Violent and unpredictable currents swirled among them.

On 30 November, the *Speedwell* entered the channel between Chiloe and mainland Chile and stood in for the harbor of Chacao, the governor's seat, wearing French colors.

When they got into the channel, the local pilot they had picked up seemed to know as little about its dangers as they did themselves. The wind freshened, bringing thick, rainy weather. A current setting from the lee of the island gripped the *Speedwell* by the bows, then another struck her under her quarter. She would not answer her helm, and the strength of the currents drove her, helpless, toward the western shore into three and a half fathoms. Here the current ran so strong and the bottom was so foul that sand floated to the surface. In thirteen fathoms Shelvocke dropped the anchor, which, mercifully, held.

But the windward tide raced, whipping up a heavy sea. The wind increased. At two in the afternoon, *Speedwell*'s cable parted, and one anchor was lost. Smartly Shelvocke shook out his topsails and stood right across the channel. A lively gale drove them southward; the holding ground beneath the pounding waves was unknown. Shelvocke looked at his charts and decided to seek shelter and replenishment at Chacao, the governor's seat, relying on his French colors. They passed two inviting but deserted bays, then, quite suddenly, as the ship rounded a high pyramid of rock, they found themselves in shelter, out of the tide. Even Betagh had to "allow Captain Shelvocke to be as able a seaman as perhaps any whatever."[1] They immediately came to.

Next morning Shelvocke sent Sam Randall away in the pinnace, well manned and armed, to locate Chacao. Hatley went in the launch, to find a watering place. The second captain's boat returned with an Indian guide, who professed to know of a good place for water and timber. He was turned around smartly with empty casks, a wood-chopping party, and an officer and ten marines for protection. They returned with sailing directions for Chacao, but also the bad news that their presence was known in Chiloe, and the Spaniards had forbidden all contact with them. The pinnace did not return at all. Shelvocke feared that he had lost her and her valuable crew.

On 3 December at seven in the evening, a big dugout canoe, called locally a piragua, rowed by eight Indians, brought a Spanish officer to check the ship's credentials. Shelvocke ordered the watch below out of sight, with only French or Spanish speakers on deck. Shelvocke assumed, with no evidence to the contrary, that France and Spain were not at war. He attempted to pass the *Speedwell* off as the French *St. Rose,* with himself as "Le Capitaine Janis le Breton," a real commander who had made several voyages in these seas.

Luckily the Spaniard's French was no better than his own. He stayed aboard and drank all night, departing with a hangover in the morning and bearing a letter from Capitaine le Breton, requesting supplies for his voyage back to France. The messenger had apparently swallowed Shelvocke's unlikely story, along with enough hipsy to float a frigate.

On 5 December, two piraguas full of armed men were sighted heading for the *Speedwell.* They took a good look at the ship and paddled past her to land armed men on a small island commanding the harbor mouth, where several cannon were mounted on a platform. Shelvocke had had some grenadiers' tall, pointed caps made up, in case of this sort of emergency.[2] He ordered the men to put them on, spread out over the ship, and look fearsome. Every five minutes the officer of the watch sang out loudly to them to keep a good lookout. They shouted out, "Aye, aye!" This was kept up throughout the night. These antics seemed to scare the Chacaons, who did not appear all day, and next night drove their cattle into the woods too far for the British to follow them. Finally a white flag was waved ashore.

Shelvocke dispatched the launch, which found a letter made fast to a flagstaff, and a dozen hams. These were a peace offering from the governor, Don Nicolas Salvo. He had become suspicious of the strange ship's bona fides when she had failed to send a boat as soon as she had anchored, to present her credentials. This was the proper procedure. His worst doubts had been confirmed when the *Speedwell*'s pinnace crew had fired upon an unarmed Spanish boat and hidden some of the governor's sheep. Assuming that Shelvocke was a pirate, the governor warned him that the whole of the Spanish-governed coast was now thoroughly alerted. He asked them to leave immediately.

To soften first impressions, Shelvocke gave the governor one and a half pounds of butter, one pound of black pepper, and two Dutch cheeses. The absence of his pinnace's crew, nine of his most trusted men, made Shelvocke increasingly uneasy. On the assumption that they were prisoners of the Spanish, he promised to leave within twenty-four hours, provided that they were returned to him. Don Nicolas replied that he did not have the men, whom he also accused of ransacking some Indian houses and kidnapping two of his Indian servants.

Convinced that pinnace and crew were lost, Shelvocke now turned to overt threats. He warned Don Nicolas, via the letter drop at the flagstaff, that he must have provisions and would take them if necessary. Still clinging to his French cover, next morning he sent First Lieutenant Brookes with twenty-nine well-armed men in the launch to take whatever provisions they could lay their hands on. Betagh and the elderly marine lieutenant Dodd were ordered ashore with a large party of marines, but no powder and shot, to intimidate the Spaniards. Betagh complained to no avail that they would need more than fresh air in their barrels to make an impression. In his growing paranoia, the Irishman was convinced that this foray was meant to provoke the Spaniards, who would most likely kill them all, as they had obviously done to the pinnace's crew. This would leave fewer witnesses to Shelvocke's excesses, with bigger shares of loot for the others.

Brookes and the launch returned in the evening with a large piragua that they had captured, both boats laden with sheep, hogs, fowls, hams, barley, green peas, and beans. Soon afterward, the missing pinnace and her thoroughly shaken crew returned to the ship. A fierce tide had carried them away, Randall explained, and they had fought their way back through several canoes of armed Indians. He and his men expressed such shame and chagrin that Shelvocke merely reprimanded the young lieutenant. Abandoning the idea of sacking Chacao, now thoroughly on the alert, he decided to get what further provisions he could from the Indian plantations and farms, which would probably be poorly defended.

Finally the ship's decks were packed with live cattle, including some guanacos or llamas, an abundance of poultry, and plenty of wheat, barley, potatoes, Indian corn (maize)—in all, Shelvocke computed, enough for four months' rations. At six in the morning on 13 December 1719, the *Speedwell* weighed and sailed out on the wings of a west-sou'westerly wind, leaving behind one deserter, Robert Morrice, who had jumped ship the night before and escaped into the woods. He was now, in all probability, revealing details of the ship's plans.

It was time to make for Juan Fernandez Island to see if Clipperton was there, or at least a message from him. But there was

Chiloean peasant stalking cattle. (J. Poolman)

opposition from the ship's company. They were very much under the influence of la Fontaine, who was now lauding the glories of the port of Concepción. But the governor of Chacao might well have sent the *Speedwell* deserter to this big, important town, by now, for interrogation. If Morrice arrived there before the *Speedwell*, he would reveal everything he knew about the English privateer masquerading as a Frenchman. More fuel would be added to the brushfire spreading all along the coast, and it would only be a matter of time before all trade there was stopped.

The lure of loot, however, was too strong for the Speedwells. In the roadstead at Concepción, la Fontaine claimed, there were always five or six sail, and others coming and going, often with money and gold and silver plate. All were weakly armed ships with no fortifications ashore to protect them. If there were twenty sail, the *Speedwell* could take them all! If there was no treasure aboard, there would be cargoes of corn, wine, brandy, flour, bread, or jerked beef, besides booty that might be taken from rich merchants. Any ship that fell into their hands could be ransomed at very great rates.

All of this was supported by Irish Will Morphew, who knew these waters and their ports well and hoped that Shelvocke would head right away for Concepción, and not let a mere formal order weigh against the idea.

In fact Shelvocke needed little persuading to put off the call at Juan Fernandez, where Clipperton might be waiting. On 23 December 1719, *Speedwell* arrived in the bay of Concepción, a large and spacious anchorage. Shelvocke took her cautiously about two miles into the bay and came to anchor in twenty-five fathoms, the anchor holding uneasily in soft black ooze. The town, founded in 1550 by Peter Baldivia, had been destroyed twice and the Spaniards driven out by the Indians. It was too dark to see if there were any ships in the offing, and Shelvocke sent the boats off to investigate and surprise any they found.

About noon, Hatley and Betagh returned and reported taking the *Solidad D'Anday* of 150 tons, the only largish vessel in the bay, recently arrived from Bolivia but with nothing on board except a few cedar planks, and nobody minding the ship but an old black bosun and two Indians. Hatley had left Brookes in charge of her, with orders to bring her down to *Speedwell* as soon as possible. On his way back to the ship, Hatley had captured a small vessel of about 25 tons near the island of Quiriquine in the harbor, where she had taken on pears, cherries, and other fruits for the Concepción market. He had chased another boat to within range of the shore batteries, which had fired on him and almost decapitated him.

The Speedwells celebrated a rather muted Christmas Day 1719, but at noon on Boxing Day, Brookes brought up the captured *Solidad D'Anday.* Her bosun told Shelvocke about a vessel laden with wines, brandy, and other valuables bound for Chiloe, anchored in the bay of Herradura, two leagues to the north of them. Randall was sent there in the fruit barque, now rechristened *Mercury* (which Betagh thought ironic for a vessel that could not be rowed and that sailed like a barge) with orders (repeated twice, as it was Randall) *not* to set foot ashore or take on anything dangerous.

But the second lieutenant seemed congenitally unable to follow orders. *Mercury* entered the bay of Herradura and found the ship in question high and dry ashore, with nothing in her hold, having landed her cargo. But the *Solidad* bosun thought he knew the warehouse where the goods must still be, and Randall sent a party ashore to attack it. The men were driven back by armed horsemen, and five of them cut down in the shallows, foretopman Jim Daniel being caught in a noose and captured. The *Mercury* had, meanwhile, grounded, so the rest were able to run to her, and the enemy retired when they came within musket range of the barque. Randall managed to get her off, and she bumped her way over sandbanks with the enemy shooting at them.

When they heard of this further misfortune, the spirits of *Speedwell*'s ship's company sank even lower. They cursed the ship, the captain, the owners, the South Sea. If this was making their fortunes, they would have done better to have stayed home and begged in the streets. It was certainly frustrating to find only one empty ship in what was normally one of the busiest ports on the coast. Discontent was rife again. The idea of India was mooted again for'ard. Some men remembered the incident of the shooting down of the albatross off the Horn, and Hatley was blamed for all their bad luck since.

Shelvocke refrained from blaming the men for forcing him to go to Concepción: "I did all I could to encourage them and to disperse the melancholy which was fixed in every countenance," he said.[3]

As he was giving Randall a tongue-lashing for his fatheaded mismanagement of the *Mercury* caper, a large ship was sighted in the offing. It was dusk, but the newcomer stood in speedily. The English privateer was already cleared for action, and she now lay at readiness to slip her cable, with the launch manned to prevent the crew of the stranger from either landing or taking the ship out again. As she came near, Shelvocke hailed her, received no reply, and fired into her, ordering the launch away. The other ship shortened sail but did not drop her anchor. Just as Shelvocke was about to slip his cable, the launch came up with the stranger, gave her a volley of small-arms fire, and the other vessel's captain came to and called for quarter.

About two in the morning, the launch returned to the *Speedwell* with the Spanish captain of the *St. Fermin,* as the victim was called, and some of her merchant passengers, who reported the three-hundred-ton vessel as being of and from Callao, with a small cargo of sugar, molasses, rice, coarse French linen, clothing, and bays from Quito, some chocolate, and about six thousand dollars in money and wrought plate.

Shelvocke took all the bales, boxes, chests, and portmanteaus out of her, and all the rice, with much of the sugar, molasses, and chocolate, about seven thousand pounds' weight of very good rusks, and all the eatables and stores that the *St. Fermin* carried. Capt. Don Francisco Larrayn pleaded for the ransoming of his ship. Shelvocke graciously agreed, and allowed Don Francisco to go in his own launch to Concepción to raise the money.

In the meantime, the *Speedwell* sailors were busy searching the prize. Every inch of her was checked for valuables, including all the pockets of passengers and crew. The carpenters were set to work to deck-in the *Mercury*, as she could be of great further use to them. Having the lines of a locally built vessel, she was not immediately recognizable as an enemy.

On 30 December, a boat under a flag of truce came out to *Speedwell*, with an officer who brought news that of the five men cut down in the rout ashore, three—John Adie, John Delly, and seaman George Alderdash—had, regrettably, died of their wounds. But the other two, including the lassoed Jim Daniel, were in a fair way to recovery, having been attended by the governor's own surgeon. The governor sent Shelvocke a present of seven jars of very good wine, the produce of the country, and informed him that the boat Hatley had chased and nearly caught had brought the news of them from Chiloe, as well as Morrice, the deserter from the *Speedwell*.

The governor asked to see Shelvocke's commission for the voyage, before he would treat for ransom of the *St. Fermin* and an exchange of prisoners. All that day the enemy appeared in large bodies of horsemen, and at night posted themselves along the shore and kept up a regular cannonade. *Speedwell*, at each turn of the sand in the hourglass, beat three rolls on the drum, and the watch shouted three "huzzas." To guard against attack by boarders, a seven-foot net was rigged above the gunwale on the main shrouds, and when the wind dropped, oars were stuck out around the ship like booms, though she was kept under way as much as possible. At midnight twelve guns were fired from the shore, and soon after that, a boat came alongside with a Jesuit priest, a Spanish lawyer, an Englishman, and a Scotsman.

Shelvocke showed his commission to the Englishman, who read out the contents in Spanish. The priest said that his purpose, apart from being a mediator to ease any friction, was to pass on the offer by the captains of the *St. Fermin* and *Solidad* of twelve thousand dollars for the ransom of both ships and the *Mercury,* instead of the sixteen thousand asked by Shelvocke for the *St. Fermin* alone.

Shelvocke then demanded sixteen thousand dollars for the two larger ships. If this was not paid within twenty-four hours, the captains would lose their ships. The delegation left at six in the morning. Shelvocke was sure that their real mission had been to inspect the ship and her strength, and he had tried to give an impression of stern ruthlessness.

As time went by, Shelvocke sent Betagh ashore, insisting that he take his servant with him wearing one of the grenadier caps. "The fellow," says Betagh, "being of a squat size looked more like a burlesque figure in a droll than a servant to an ambassador."[4]

The governor, pleased that the English ship was properly commissioned and not one of the pirates who had treated them so barbarously in the past, received the Irishman civilly. The captain of the *St. Fermin,* he said, had his money already counted to send out to the *Speedwell.* But, as Betagh had feared, the tall grenadier cap of his servant, with yellow facings, gave great offense, being taken as a deliberate ridicule of a bishop's miter, which was all the more outrageous on the head of the toad-like little tar.

Two days passed without any further word from the governor, and Shelvocke became convinced that he had something in mind quite other than the payment of ransom. Then, on 4 January 1720, the two wounded men were returned, with a letter from the governor repeating the offer of the twelve thousand dollars originally offered for the ships.

Shelvocke promptly burned the *Solidad.* Next day brought another letter from the governor offering twelve thousand dollars for the *St. Fermin.* Shelvocke replied that he "could no longer trust those who had dealt so ambiguously with me as under a pretence of acting in an honourable manner, to be not privately plotting and contriving how they might destroy us." He threatened that if he had not received the twelve thousand dollars by the following noon, the *St. Fermin* would go the way of the *Solidad.*

Yet another letter from the governor promised the money, but not until the following morning. It was difficult, he said, to raise the sum, because nearly all the people of the town had sent their money away on hearing of the English ship in their waters.

Shelvocke extended the deadline until the following noon. There was no news in the forenoon; noon passed, and Shelvocke made preparations for sailing, loosening his sails and at the same time unfurling all the *St. Fermin*'s sails. He hoisted a Spanish jack at her fore-topmast head and a Spanish ensign at her main-topmast head, to hasten any last-minute rush with the money. The afternoon wore on, and seeing no boat of any kind coming out to them, Shelvocke ordered the *St. Fermin* put to the torch. Her loose cotton sails made a great blaze, and the *Speedwell* got under way. The governor had obviously wanted to delay matters long enough to warn all the other ports on the coast and, possibly, call up Spanish warships. Shelvocke hoped that the burning of the *Solidad* and *St. Fermin* would be a warning to other governors and captains to pay ransoms without delay.

6

Mercury's War

IN THE forenoon of 8 January aboard the *Speedwell*, heading for Juan Fernandez, Chief Mate Stewart, ship's company agent, began the unenviable job of weighing the money and plate from the *St. Fermin.* Shelvocke ordered Hendry, originally the owners' agent and later rated purser by Shelvocke, to take strict account of everything in the interests of the Gentlemen Adventurers. Stewart also sold plunder at the mast, at very extravagant prices.

The men would not allow Hendry any part in the appraisal of the plunder, but they did not hinder him from recording the transactions. Betagh twice tried to form a party to oppose the owners' having nothing but what was freight or mentioned on bills of lading. He told Shelvocke that to withhold anything else from them would be completely unjust. But Shelvocke said he was afraid that the men would then decide to describe everything taken as plunder. However, he reminded them of the terms of their own St. Catherine's articles, which meant hardship enough to the owners. Not plate nor money nor anything else of high value taken out of the *St. Fermin* was mentioned on any bill of lading or any other document, except some large silver candlesticks for the church at Concepción, everything else having been found in cabins or private chests.

Betagh could raise no support. Shelvocke wondered what would happen if they met the *Success.*

With everything accounted for and the value of shares calculated, the crew asked Shelvocke to give them their dividends immediately, in accordance with the St. Catherine's articles, which he could not oppose. Prize money and plunder amounting to ten pieces of eight per share (two pounds, twenty-five pence today) were distributed. All bales of coarse cotton cloth, bays, linen, ribbons, lace, silk, and other wares were equally divided, half to the owners, half to the ship's company.

The archipelago of Juan Fernandez lies in the Pacific Ocean, four hundred miles west of the port of Valparaiso in Chile, to which the archipelago belongs. It was discovered by the Spaniard Juan Fernandez in 1563–72. The largest island of the group, about thirteen miles long, was called for many years Mas a Tierra (closer to land) or, more commonly, Juan Fernandez Island. The smaller Isla Santa Clara, or Goat Island, about five miles in circumference, lies six cables (twelve hundred yards) off the southwest tip of Mas a Tierra. Ninety miles west of these two lies Mas a Fuera (further away) Island, some six miles long.

The eastern part of Juan Fernandez consists of tree-covered craggy ridges and fertile valleys. The western section is flat, low, and almost barren. Bahia Cumberland (Cumberland Bay) is the safest and best anchorage on the island. It was on Juan Fernandez Island that Alexander Selkirk was marooned. Daniel Defoe modeled his hero Robinson Crusoe on Selkirk. Confusingly, in 1974–75, the Chilean government renamed Juan Fernandez Isla Robinson Crusoe, and Mas a Fuera Isla Alejandro Selkirk.[1]

At six o'clock on the morning of 11 January 1720, they sighted Mas a Tierra. There *Mercury* was beached to plug her leaks. In the bark of a big tree near the landing place, one man noticed the inscription "W. Magee, 1719." Magee was the name of the *Success*'s surgeon, suggesting that Clipperton had called here. Shelvocke sailed again on the 15 January, well stocked up once more with provisions and all water casks filled. He made what speed he could to the northward.

On 5 February, Shelvocke sent *Mercury* on ahead with Brookes and Rainer, first lieutenant of marines, to scout for shipping in the port of Arica. *Speedwell* sighted the headland of Arica and the island of Guano, with a ship at anchor on the north side of it, just as the *Mercury* came forging out of the bay as if a whole Spanish squadron had been after her.

Shelvocke was pleasantly surprised to find that the ship, the *Rosario,* one hundred tons, had been taken. But his feelings changed when the wind veered and brought the smell of the cargo wafting aboard *Speedwell.* It was cormorants' dung, called guano, with which the ship was loaded. Young ensign Hamilton of the marine contingent kept a journal, and he put his entry for the day into Scottish vernacular: "This geud day we a taen a smal vashel lodded wi turd."[2]

But the dung boat had some value: her cargo, brought from the island of Iquique, was used for the cultivation of agi (cod-pepper) in the vale of Arica. Shelvocke demanded ransom for her.

Soon after this, the *Speedwell* took a vessel of about ten tons as she sailed into the roadstead with a cargo of dead fish and guano. Arica had formerly been famous for the gold and silver plate exported, but had now been reduced in circumstances. It looked like ancient ruins, except for its church. As soon as it as dark, the owner of the *Rosario,* Miguel Diaz Gonsalez, came aboard the *Speedwell.* Shelvocke asked 1,500 pieces of eight (33,750 pounds today) for the ship and her crew of six negroes, having already taken out of her anything that looked useful. Gonsalez pleaded poverty and a large family to feed. But twenty-four hours later, he brought the whole amount, 1,300 dollars' value in ingots of virgin silver called *pinnas,* and the rest in pieces of eight.

Shelvocke shaped course for Hilo, which was sighted at three

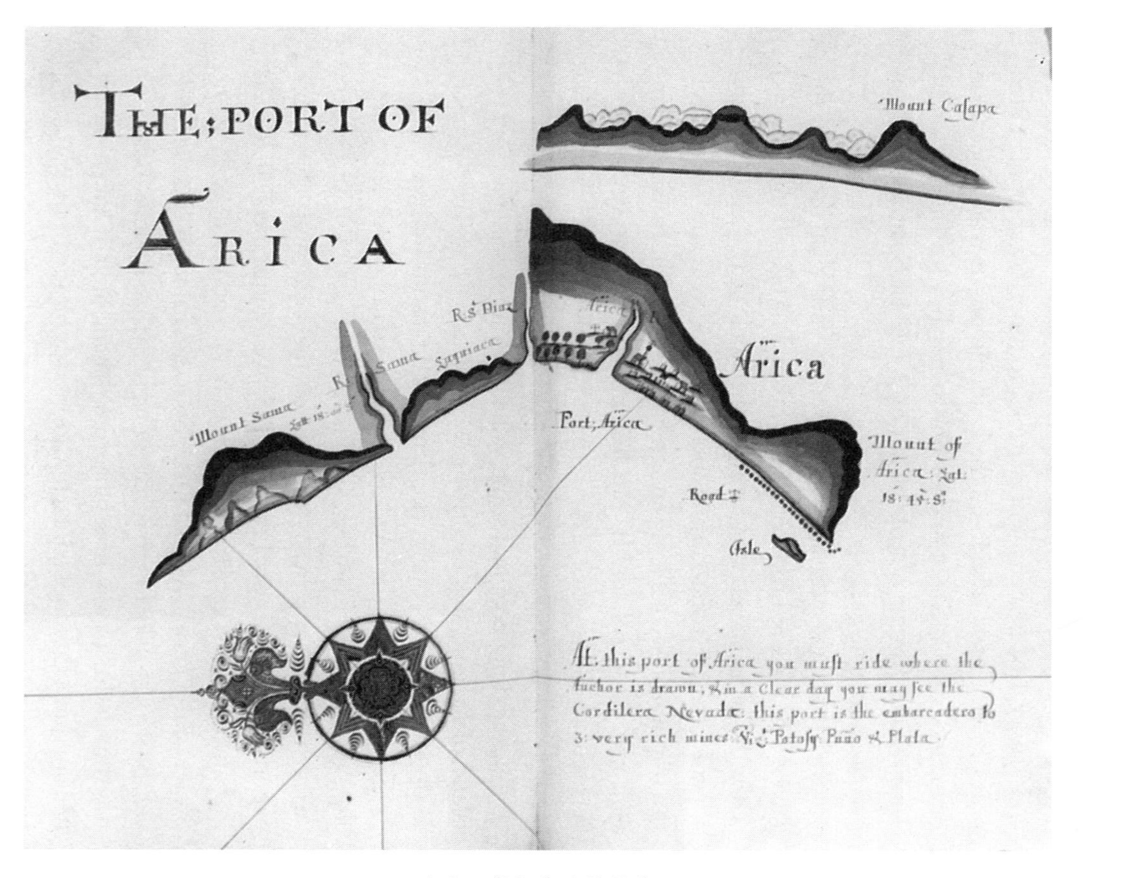

Arica. (Hack, NMM)

in the afternoon next day, with one large and three small ships at anchor there. The big ship hoisted French colors, and Shelvocke recognized her as the *Sage Solomon* from St. Catherine's. She proceeded to fire four shots at him. He immediately brought to, to consider his course of action. He could turn the *Mercury* into a "brander" (fireship). But Britain was not at war with France. Provoked though he had been, an incident might cause serious trouble in Europe. He clapped the helm aweather, and, mindful of the *Sage Solomon*'s forty guns, stood out to sea again, preferring discretion to valor.

In the forenoon of 12 February, the crew had the money taken at Arica divided among them, according to their number of shares. Ten days later the ship was abreast of Callao, the port for Lima, the Peruvian capital. But prospects here looked poor, and *Speedwell* slipped away in the night on the wings of a stiff breeze.

On 26 February, Sim Hatley suggested taking the *Mercury* along the coast. He had previously traveled from Lima to Payta by land, and he had passed through several prosperous towns that traded with Lima via small ships, which often carried rich goods.

Shelvocke could only approve of the scheme. They might well also meet the Panama treasure ships, always inshore in the evenings to get the benefit of offshore winds, which blew all night and most of the morning.

Hatley's plan cheered everybody up. Shelvocke increased *Mercury*'s crew, gave them a month's provisions, mounted two of *Speedwell*'s quarterdeck guns in her, lent Hatley the pinnace, and gave him a copy of their commission, with full orders and instructions, though it seemed fairly certain that they would see him before the time of the appointed rendezvous in the Lobos Islands, some sixty leagues away. *Mercury,* with Betagh as second in command, cast off. Her crew gave Shelvocke three hearty cheers, and she stood right in for the shore.

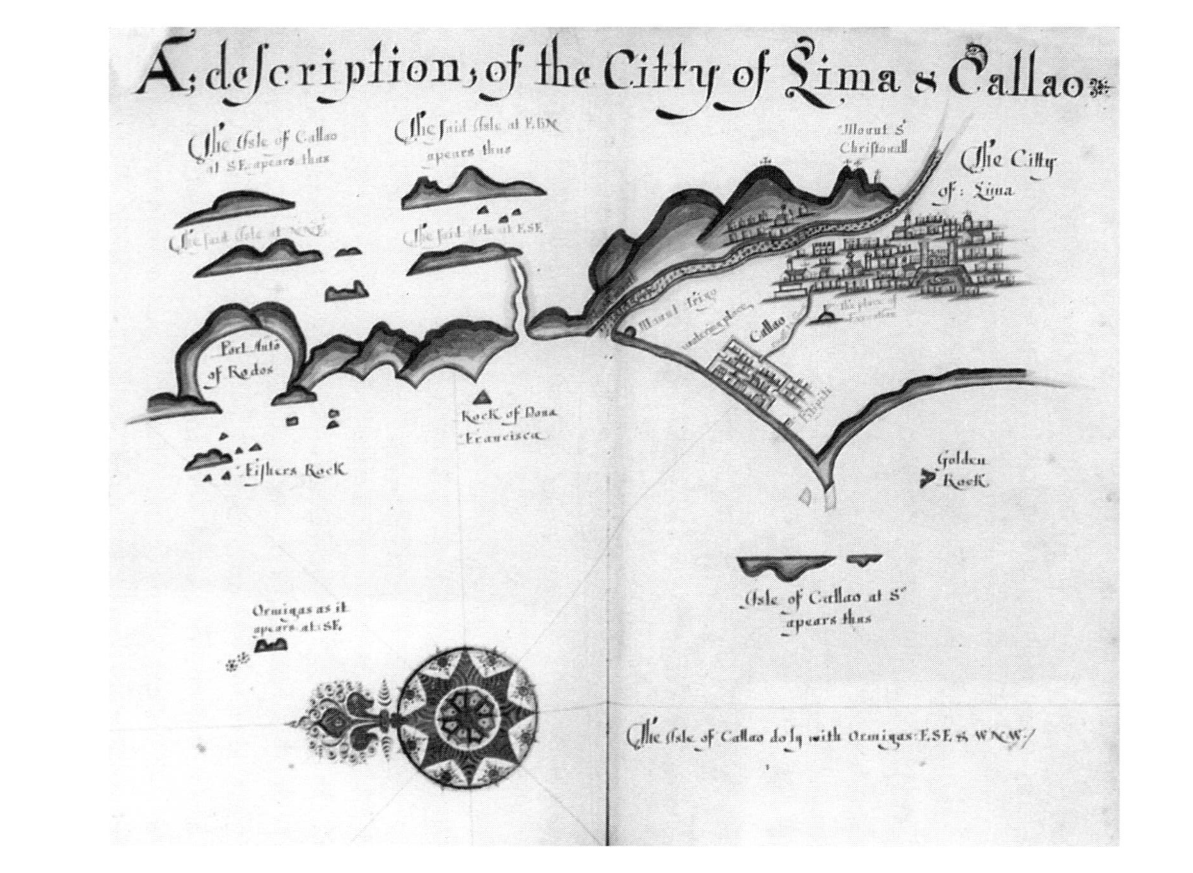

Lima and Callao. (Hack, NMM)

The very next morning, *Mercury* captured a small barque laden with rice, chocolate, wheat, and flour, and next day she took another, similarly loaded. On 4 March they took a "pink," worth 150,000 dollars, a handsome, well-found vessel. Flushed with this success, Betagh persuaded Hatley and most of the men not to return to the *Speedwell.* They had captured loot enough to set themselves up as gentlemen for the rest of their lives, but the owners would take most of that, with the remainder divided up into five hundred shares.

As fortune had favored them, they would be foolish if they did not take the chance of sailing to India. They had enough provisions and everything else needed for the voyage, including Captain Hatley, who could certainly navigate them to the coast of Asia. The Irishman's eloquent blarney carried the day. The resolution was adopted, and all but a few hands transferred to the big pink, keeping the *Mercury* in company.

Hatley, however, pondered the implications of the action. The proposed voyage carried many risks and dangers. Even if they reached India, his own treachery might well be discovered, and he could never show his face in England again. He remembered how Clipperton had suffered after he had deserted Dampier to run away with one of his prizes. He did not know what to do—whether to follow Shelvocke, which was his duty, or the slippery Betagh. This was mutiny, not to mention outright piracy on the high seas.

His mood of uncertainty spread to the men, and the two vessels hovered off the coast, following a haphazard course. But Betagh plied the second captain with drink. In the end he opted for India and the riches of the Orient. But some of the dissenters got quietly into the pinnace and shoved off, ready to surrender to the enemy rather than cross the line into buccaneering.

The mutineers had also neglected to mount a proper lookout while the argument was going on, and no sooner had they clapped their helm aweather for the broad Pacific than they sighted a sail standing toward them. There was no way for either ship, especially the flat-bottomed *Mercury,* to avoid this fast sailer, which turned out to be one of the Spanish men-o'-war activated to look for the English pirates. It was the forty-gun *Brilliant,* flagship of the Spanish admiral Don Pedro Miranda.

As the enemy approached, Betagh and Hatley in the pink dressed themselves in some of the Spanish clothes they found below, confined the passengers closely in the great cabin, hoisted the Spanish colors, and allowed only Indians and Negroes out on deck. The charade might well have succeeded, had it not been for gunner's mate John Sprake.

As the Spanish admiral came up with them, Hatley lowered his topsails. He hoped his Spanish would not be tested too rigorously. The Spanish captain called out, "Have you heard anything of the English privateer?"

"No."

"Why have you got no further in your voyage to Lima?"

"The currents."

After several more questions, the Spanish admiral seemed satisfied and was about to shove off again, when Sprake and two more men appeared on the pink's main deck. A French lookout in the *Brilliant* saw three pairs of unmistakable British bell-bottoms. His shrill shout rang out, "Dieu, monsieur, ils sont Anglois!"[3]

Brilliant fired a broadside of round and partridge shot into them at once, one shot slightly wounding Hatley in the head. He had no option but to surrender. The Spaniard then sank the *Mercury* and rescued the crew.

The English Protestants were treated roughly, especially Sim Hatley, who had on him when he was searched 96 moidores (130 pounds). The Spaniards accused him of seizing them from the Cape Frio ship, and he was put in irons. The Irish Betagh was assumed to be a Roman Catholic, though he had actually embraced the Church of England some years before. He was treated with special hospitality when it came out that he knew, or said he knew, Capt. Sir Charles Wager, a British privateer who had once taken Don Pedro prisoner and treated him with great courtesy. After that, Betagh dined at the admiral's table.

Betagh, surgeon's mate Pressick, and marine sergeant Cobb were sent to Piura, where Betagh spent six weeks in the mansion of the Spanish St. Bueno family, Hatley and the others being taken to Lima on mule back. This was a hard journey of four hundred miles, during which bosun Laming of the *Speedwell* died. Betagh and Pressick were next taken on mules to Payta, where *Brilliant* had just put in after a fruitless search for the *Speedwell.* Betagh and Pressick cruised with her to Callao, Betagh being presented with a handsome suit of clothes, two pairs of silk stockings, a hat, wig, and shirts by *Brilliant*'s captain. After a five-week cruise they were put ashore and incarcerated with the other *Speedwell* prisoners, including Hatley, who was in solitary confinement. They all appeared before a judge's court charged with piracy, but only Hatley was found guilty, with Shelvocke named as the principal in the crime. Hatley was lucky to get away with twelve months in irons.

Most of the English prisoners embraced the Catholic faith, which brought them "good meat and drink and a quiet life," one man said—a true English matelot. Twelve of them were sent to Callao to help careen and refit the frigate *Flying Fish,* and they formed a plan to take the ship *Margarita,* led by John Sprake. Betagh declined to join and the plot was discovered, but, once again, the gentle archbishop and viceroy Don Diego Merfilia had them all released except Sprake. He spent three months in irons.

Betagh later denied that he had actually accepted an officer's commission in the *Brilliant,* but he admitted that he had kept his watch on board. This was in return, he insisted, for the gentlemanly way in which he had been treated by the Spaniards—as far less of an enemy than by his former captain, who had called him a traitor. Practically all Hatley's men were employed working the admiral's flagship. Pressick acted as her surgeon for wages. By way of further payment, Betagh revealed as much as he knew of Shelvocke's behavior on the voyage and of his future plans, which would result, he hoped, in the *Speedwell*'s capture very soon. He relished the thought, and asked Don Pedro to give him the honor of being the first man aboard her when she was taken.

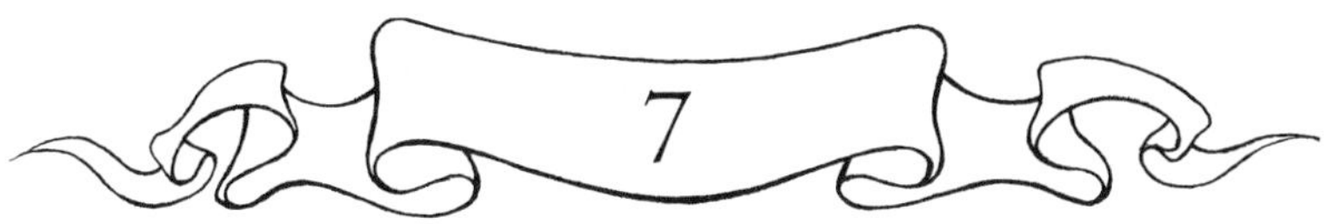

7

Rocks and Roundshot

At first light on 29 February 1720, the *Speedwell* was off the roadstead of Guanchaco, where she saw a ship at anchor. At eleven o'clock she eased alongside her. She was the *Carmensita,* one hundred tons, with nothing in her except a little timber from Guayaquil, and only two Indians and a boy to guard her. They told Shelvocke of a rich ship in the cove of Payta that had put in there to repair some gale damage. Shelvocke immediately put to sea, but in raising the anchor, *Carmensita*'s cable parted. His prize was new and well fitted out and promised to be a good sailer, so he renamed her the *St. David* and took her into his service, thus becoming a commodore of sorts. He intended to convert her into a brander once the *Mercury* was back, and the incendiary equipment he had put into her had been transferred.

On 2 March *Speedwell* was within three leagues of Lobos de Tierra, the prearranged rendezvous with the *Mercury.* Standing into the road and not seeing her there, Shelvocke sent Randall ashore with two crosses to be set up over two bottles buried in the sand. Each contained a letter to Hatley, in which Shelvocke mentioned information from the *Carmensita* men that another English ship had taken several prizes on the coast. It seemed possible that this was the *Success.* By this time, of course, *Mercury* was gone. Betagh was haunting the bows of *Brilliant,* searching the horizon for *Speedwell*'s pestered top-hamper.

Shelvocke continued coasting to the northward. He had now

come to believe that the *Mercury* was lost. Hatley and Betagh, both unreliable men and potential mutineers, he would not miss, but they had taken fourteen of his best seamen with them—John Sprake, Robert Copps, bosun Laming, Matt Appleton, John Wilson, Jack Panther, Christopher Prestwick, Martin Hayden, Robert Bowman, Edward Nately, Will Dobson, Richard Gloins, and Tom Barnet, as well as the young ensign Hamilton.

On 21 March they entered the cove of Payta, flying French colors once again. There was a small ship at anchor there, her foremast out and her main-topmast unrigged. At the sight of *Speedwell* a boat came out from shore toward the unrigged ship, and Shelvocke sent Brookes in the launch to stop them from carrying off anything of value to the town. The first lieutenant soon returned, having left Stewart and five men in the prize. They found nothing but timber and a little jerked beef. *Speedwell* came to an anchor, before it got dark, in seven fathoms about three-quarters of a mile from the town. But they had to leave the *St. David* to cruise off the Saddle of Payta, as she had no anchors.

The taking of Payta was part of the original plan drawn up by the Gentlemen Adventurers, and Shelvocke consulted with his officers on the best method of attack. The place was large, populous, and important, a rendezvous for most ships from Panama and Callao, and he could expect opposition. At two o'clock in the dark middle watch, Shelvocke himself landed with forty-six men, leaving Blowfield Coldsea to bring the ship gradually nearer in, to make it easier to embark plunder. The party marched up to the big church without being checked, and they found the town deserted except for an old Indian and a boy. They told them that an English captain had put prisoners ashore here some time previously but had made no serious attempt to take the king's treasure. At first light they saw great bodies of men gathered in the hills on either side of them, who, Shelvocke anticipated, would rush them as soon as they saw their puny strength. But as the Speedwells, wearing grenadiers' caps and looking as fierce as possible, marched up the hill toward them, they fell back, having taken with them part of the king's treasure, amounting to four hundred thousand pieces of eight (ninety thousand pounds).

Suddenly the advancing jack-tars heard a cannon fire in the harbor. Shelvocke at once halted and sent a man to find out what it meant. He returned with the news that the *Speedwell* was aground. The sailors returned to the boats, and the enemy came running down from the hills, whooping with bravado. Shelvocke rushed aboard ship, which was afloat but within her own width of the rocks. Coldsea, with very little wind in which to maneuver, had been caught in stays, with the wind pushing on the front surfaces of the sails. While he was trying to fill his sails again, it suddenly fell dead calm, and he was almost aground before he could drop an anchor. The water being smooth, Shelvocke soon warped her off again, then returned to take possession of the town, with the enemy running back into the hills.

They spent the rest of the day shipping what plunder they had got, including hogs, calavance beans, Indian corn, wheat, flour, sugar, and as much coconut as they could stow away. In the afternoon Shelvocke sent a messenger, demanding 10,000 pieces of eight (2,250 pounds) for the town and the ship, to be paid within twenty-four hours. The governor refused to ransom the town. He said he did not care what Shelvocke did with it, provided he spared the churches. Shelvocke threatened that the whole town, without exception, would be reduced to ashes, and gave the ship's captain three hours to produce ransom for the ship, or she would be burned.

The Spaniards did not appear to grasp the urgency of the matter or appreciate that the English captain meant what he said. What Shelvocke did not know was that they had sighted the Spanish man-o'-war *Peregrine,* fifty guns, on the other side of the island and had directed her to the enemy vessel in the roadstead. During the night the Spaniard crept to within a league of the entrance to the cove, under cover of the high land mass, and the English lookouts did not see her until she was within gunshot of them.

Meanwhile, having got no satisfaction from the town, Shelvocke had ordered it set on fire in several places. The houses were very flammable and blazed away fiercely. But no sooner was all Payta afire than Shelvocke received frantic signals from the *Speedwell* to rejoin her, and she opened a continuous fire upon the harbor entrance. Shelvocke ordered all hands back to the ship. He himself took off in a canoe with three men. He had got about halfway across when he saw the unmistakable lines of a large Spanish vessel, with her high fo'c'sle and poop, the Spanish ensign at the foretopmast head.

A battle was clearly under way, and Blowfield Coldsea had won the first round decisively, having opened fire on the Spaniard so smartly and so thoroughly frightened her scratch crew that many deserted their posts. Her Creole captain overestimated the weight of *Speedwell*'s broadside, so that he wasted time preparing as if to fight a seventy-four, giving Shelvocke a chance to get back on board and mount more guns, loosen all sails, and make all other necessary preparations to meet a ship that overwhelmingly outgunned him. He badly needed the cannon he had put ashore, which the officers still there were taking far too long in getting out to him.

Peregrine's captain had to spend too much time driving his men back to their posts. The helmsman had quit the helm, so that the ship, close-hauled for standing in, came to with her headsails in the wind and muzzled herself, bobbing up and down in the water, her sails flapping against the mast. Thus she allowed all the *Speedwell* men to get back to the ship, though the two ships were within

Spanish fifty-gun warship. (MoD)

pistol range of one another before the last man had scrambled aboard. Shelvocke promptly cut their anchor cable, but the ship's head fell off the wrong way. When he braced the yards and got the sails to draw, he had only just enough room to pass the enemy.

The sheer size of the looming Spanish ship struck fear into the Speedwells. One man jumped overboard and swam ashore, and others looked as if they were about to follow his example, so great was the disproportion between the heavily gunned enemy vessel and the crank old *Speedwell,* with only six guns mounted. Being under the enemy's lee, Shelvocke managed to get into shoal water, only to lose all wind from his sails and become becalmed.

For about an hour the two ships maneuvered clumsily, with *Peregrine*'s shot often too high to hit *Speedwell*'s hull, though seriously chopping up her rigging, and the Spaniard neglecting to make effective use of his small arms to clear *Speedwell*'s fo'c'sle, waist, and quarterdeck. This was mainly because so many of his men had fled to the hold and others were on their knees praying. Whenever he was ready to fire a broadside, he gave his ship starboard helm to bring as many of his guns as possible to bear on *Speedwell* and at the same time try to shut her out of the wind. Shelvocke made the briskest return of fire he could with his few guns, but all his small arms had been taken ashore and had got wet in the hasty return, and for some time they were of no use.

Boarders were expected every minute. On hearing a sudden loud burst of shouting from the enemy and seeing his fo'c'sle full of men, a fierce-looking mob of Spaniards, Indians, mestizos, and Negroes, Shelvocke thought that the time had come. Then he saw that the hoorays were all for the shooting down of the *Speedwell*'s ensign and staff, which trailed in the water and gave the Spaniards the impression that the English ship had surrendered. Shelvocke soon undeceived them, by spreading a new ensign in the mizzen shrouds.

At last, in an attempt to finish off the obstinate Britisher once and for all, the Spanish captain clapped his helm well astarboard to bring the whole broadside to bear, but this volley had little effect. The *Speedwell* was only lightly damaged, and the enemy was unable to repeat the salvo. The enemy's sails would not draw, which gave Shelvocke time to get both ahead and to windward of her before her sails filled again. *Speedwell*'s masts, by this time only weakly supported by rigging, continued to bear what sail she had aboard and gave her a fair chance of getting clear. The Spaniard was then in a frenzy to get her spritsail yard fore and aft to make a bridge for her boarding party, all the while pounding *Speedwell* with her bow-mounted forechase gun. But the *Speedwell* was soon out of reach, and all hands put to repairing the battle damage.

Astonishingly, the *Speedwell* had not one single man killed or wounded, even when a shot came though a port, dismounted a gun between decks, and burst into sharp shards, flying fore and aft through the mass of sweating men. The Spanish ship always loomed high over the *Speedwell,* and although the latter's stern was shattered, most of the enemy's shot had continued to go high, with the result that rigging and sails had been considerably disabled. The mainmast was badly dented yet had stood up for a long time, with only one good shroud to support it. The foremast had fared little better, yet the ship kept all her canvas except the main topgallant sail at "hard bat's end" (all sails fully spread, without reefs). An unlucky shot hit the bows of the launch as she lay off the quarter and set fire to some powder cartridges that had been negligently left in her. This blew away her moorings, and she was lost. When Shelvocke saw the smoke from this arise on the quarter, he at first thought the ship was on fire.

In about an hour and a half, *Speedwell* was well clear of the Spaniard, and the *Peregrine* tacked and stood in for Payta, whereupon *Speedwell* shortened sail. No ship could have had a narrower escape, considering the odds, and it was mainly because of Shelvocke's ship handling. The loss of the launch and another anchor was serious: there was only one anchor left, and no boats at all.

At five that evening, a sail was sighted under the lee bow, which Shelvocke thought must be the *St. David.* He stood to windward all night, and next morning the single ship had become two. Shelvocke tacked and stood toward them, and soon one of them turned and headed for Payta, while the other kept stemming them. The nearer she approached, the less Shelvocke liked the look of her, and he exercised discretion by turning about and crowding on all sail. But the pursuer gained on them and drew close enough to reveal her Spanish lines. She was in fact the *Brilliant,* and it looked as if Will Betagh was going to see his dearest wish come true.

The *Brilliant* was making almost two feet to *Speedwell*'s one. There was a series of calms throughout the heat of the day, but with every little breeze the Spaniard drew closer. When night came on Shelvocke made use of an old trick that he thought might not be known in these waters: turning a light adrift in a half-tub and darkening one part of the lantern to give an intermittent light, as if the tub was a ship. *Speedwell* streamed the decoy and altered course. As day broke she handed all sail, and when full daylight came, there was nothing to be seen of the pursuer.

Speedwell kept an offing of thirty leagues (ninety miles) from the coast and was brought to, while Shelvocke took stock of their situation. He knew nothing of the *St. David*'s fate. In fact Hopkins, her commander, had put in to a coastal settlement and surrendered to Indians. John Gundy of Plymouth had had his throat cut for not stripping immediately when ordered to. The rest, along with *Mercury*'s men, were prisoners at Lima.

The viceroy had placed an embargo on all northern leeward shipping for six months. *Speedwell* had only one anchor and no boats. Nevertheless, Shelvocke intended to try his luck at Guayaquil, where, he had been informed, several big ships of value lay, under the embargo.

Calling his officers together, he pointed out the much better prospects of captures to windward—which would be unexpected, sailing south—than to leeward, with the embargo in force there. And they should be able to stay clear of the Spanish men-o'-war, while they would have the whole Chilean coast to range on. Having beat up the seven hundred leagues to windward to water at Juan Fernandez, they could cruise the whole season off Concepción, Valparaiso, and Coquimbo among the windward traders, who would supply them with anchors, cable, boats, and a ship to use as a brander. He also proposed to take Coquimbo or the town of La Serena. This was agreed, and *Speedwell* stretched to windward with a new suit of sails.

With their success in beating off the *Peregrine* and outsmarting the *Brilliant*, the holds full of provisions and loot and a good pros-

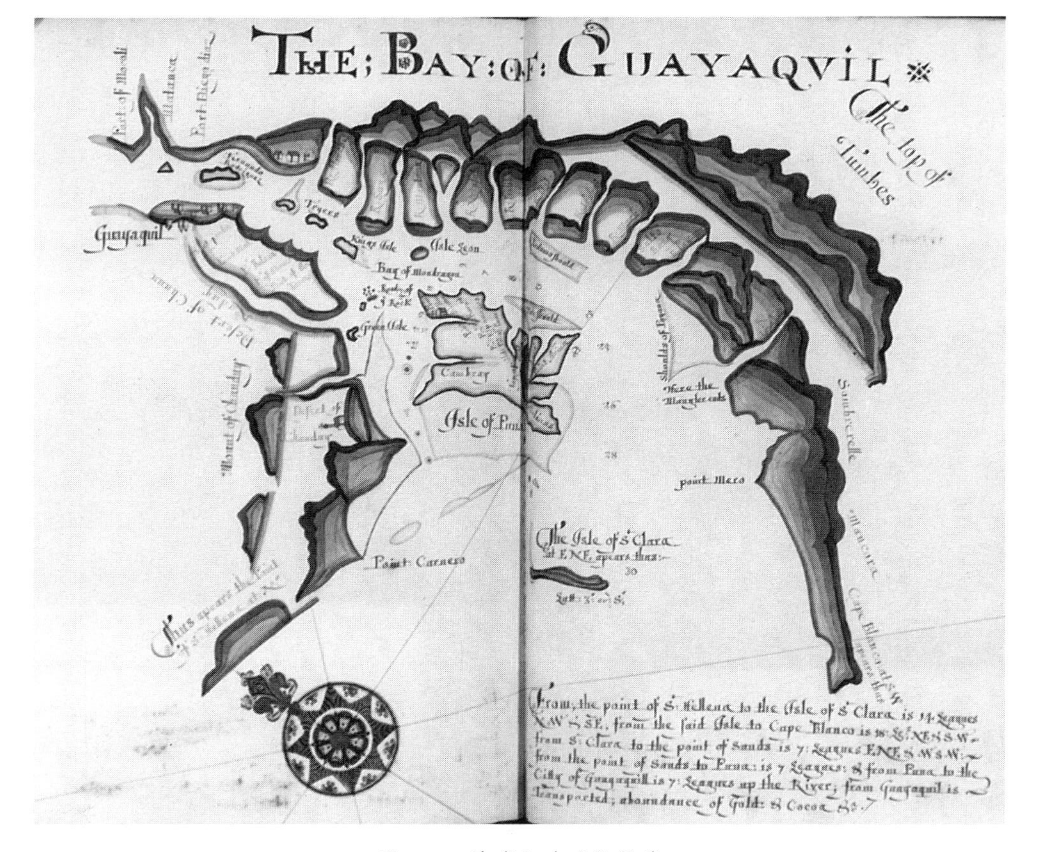

Guayaquil. (Hack, NMM)

pect of more to come, morale in the ship was at a peak. After the campaign off the coast of Chile, Shelvocke intended to sail north for the Tres Marias and California for some good wooding and watering.

And in these waters, *Speedwell* would be well placed to lie in the track of the Manila galleon, the jewel of their hopes. If they missed her, there were always the Peruvian ships bringing silver to Acapulco, and a chance to take the Indian and Chinese goods that the Manila ship brought back. Meanwhile the burgoo kettle whistled cheerfully, and each man had a quart of chocolate and three ounces of excellent rusk for breakfast every morning. They had fresh meat or fish each day—so many kept company with the ship that there was a choice between dolphin and albacore.

There was some alarm on 31 March, when pumping ship produced an unusually great discharge of water from the well, colored an inky black. This suggested a leak in the powder room. When they entered it they heard the water come in like a little sluice, and they found the best part of their powder spoiled, with only six barrels saved. It was lucky that they were experiencing fair weather, otherwise it would have been a hard matter for them to have kept the old *Speedwell* afloat.

A leak was found on the starboard side under the lower cheek of the head, caused by a shot that had lodged there, then fallen out. The ship was hove to, and the hole, with some difficulty, was stopped up.

With slightly less rosy optimism, the Speedwells picked up their course for Juan Fernandez. On 6 May they raised the westernmost islands of the archipelago, seven leagues northeast-by-north. Next day the carpenter's party completed a new yawl, big enough to carry three hogsheads. On 11 May they sighted Mas a Tierra. Here the new boat plied to and fro until the twenty-first, though it was impossible to make intake match consumption of water.

Shelvocke decided to anchor in the roadstead nearer the shore for a few hours, and he prepared twenty tons of casks to raft ashore. He worked the ship in and anchored in the best spot he could find, in forty fathoms, and made fast a warp the length of four hawsers to the rocks, to steady the ship and to use for hauling the casks ashore and back.

They were ready to go to sea next forenoon, but the weather would not permit it. *Speedwell* tossed uneasily for four days. Then, on 25 May, an unusually ferocious gale of wind blew in out of the ocean, bringing with it a great tumbling swell.

A few hours later, the cable parted. Shelvocke saw at once that there was "not the least prospect of avoiding immediate destruction."[1] The *Speedwell* was hurled on to the rocks, with everyone on deck holding fast to anything solid that came to hand. Otherwise, the violent shock as she struck would have pitched them all into the sea. Foremast, mainmast, and mizzen topmast all fell together.

8

Jamaica Discipline

SHELVOCKE FOUND some small satisfaction in reflecting that if the ship had struck just a cable's length east or west of where she hit the rocks, they would almost certainly all have drowned. As it was the masts all fell on the off side, which gave them room to make a raft and save all the men on board except seaman John Hannah, who was drowned.

The men already ashore came down to help their shipmates on to dry land, and Shelvocke himself had a very narrow escape from drowning when he went below to get his commission scroll and the chest containing eleven hundred dollars of the owners' money. He remembered how Dampier had been thrown into a stinking Dutch jail as a pirate after he had lost his letter of marque. Shelvocke also managed to get up the dry powder from the bread room and eight bags of bread, as the ship did not disintegrate immediately, though waterlogged a few minutes after she had struck.

Everyone was ashore before it was quite dark. Their only shelter from the lashing wind and rain was the cover of the trees. Mingling with the wind was the melancholy howling of innumerable seals on the beach and the fiercer barking of the great sea lions, over fifteen feet in length and weighing a ton. All were so thickly clustered that the Speedwells had to beat a way through as they stumbled along, with nothing in view but rocky precipices, inhospitable woods dripping with rain, high mountaintops hidden in thick cloud, and a tempestuous sea. The only seat was the cold, wet ground, which was also their bed for that first miserable night.

Shelvocke and the officers consulted as to how to bring off some necessities from the wreck, if she was still more or less intact in the morning. He realized that they would have to act swiftly, before she did go. They lit a fire, wrapped themselves up in whatever bits and pieces of clothing they had with them, and lay down with little hope of sleeping. Their spirits sank as they considered the small hope of rescue by a passing ship. Exhausted, however, by the struggle from the wreck to the rocks, they all fell asleep almost immediately. Like Crusoe on his desolate island, Shelvocke slept as comfortably as, he believed, few could have in his circumstances. He found himself surprisingly refreshed when first light crept through the trees.

Shelvocke awoke first, shivering with the cold. A dismal wailing came from the beach, where the seals and fierce-whiskered sea lions lay in hundreds, still airing their fear and rage. Some bleated like lambs, others howled like dogs or wolves. He looked around him. The fire that had soothed his sodden, exhausted body into deep sleep was ashes and dead embers. It was spring back in England, but here in the Southern Ocean, winter was drawing on. The sudden onshore gale that had wrecked the *Speedwell* was one of its precursors.

He looked seaward. The wild wind was still blowing, scything across the bay. It was like the wind of his life's ill luck, the wind that after the good years—the steady climb from fo'c'sle hand to the queen's warrant to full lieutenant—had blown him ashore to starve and scratch a living. It was the wind that had killed his Susannah and left him to feed young George on the charity from rare pilotage jobs in the Thames, until Hughes and the Gentlemen Adventurers had given him the *Speedwell* and a second chance

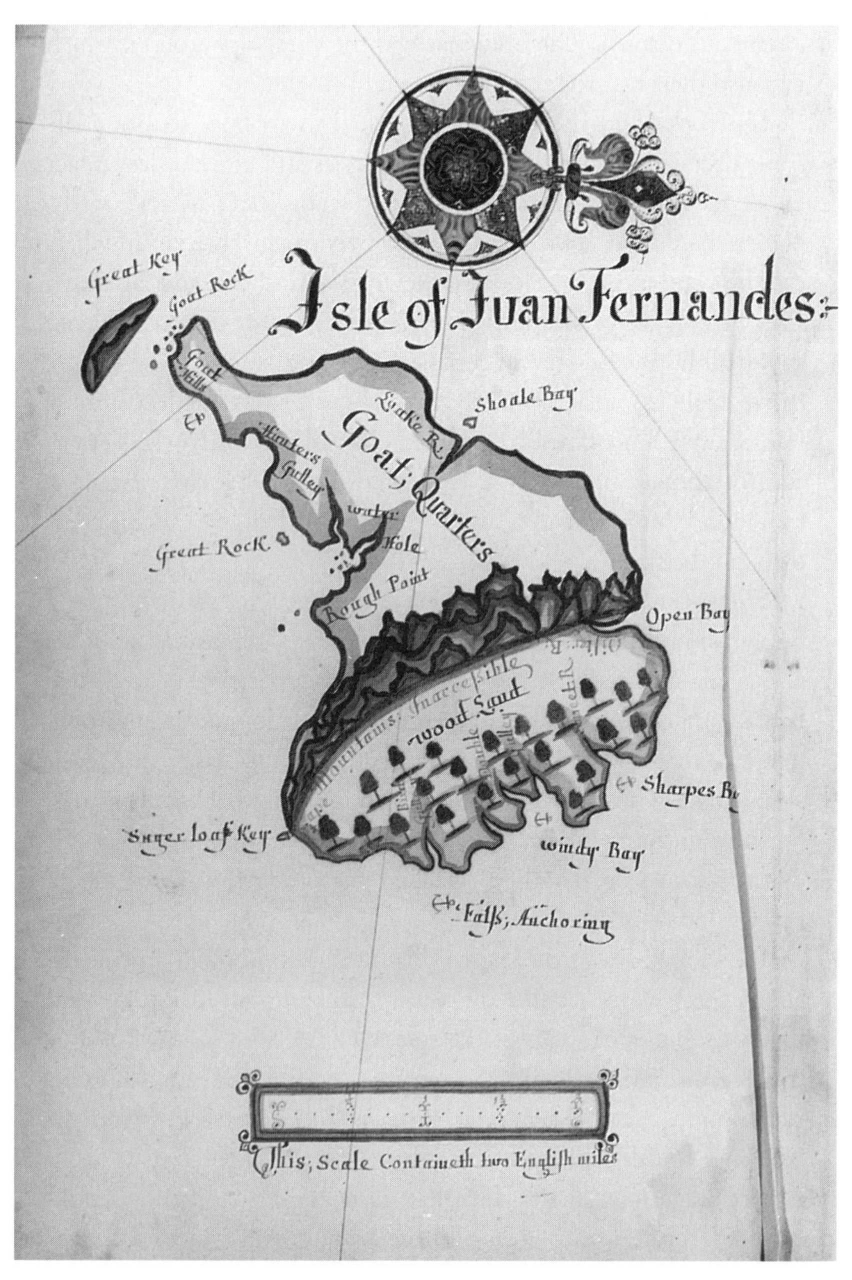

Juan Fernandez Island. (Hack, NMM)

of fortune, perhaps fame, if he could catch and take the Manila galleon. . . .

The wind raised the sheltered waters. The wreck lifted on each roller and struck the fanged rocks. He could hear the grinding and rending, carried in on the wind.

He rose. There were things to be done, work to be started on the daunting task of survival, the saving of their lives. There was food to be divided, shelter to be organized. He looked down the beach. There was the lash-up raft at the water's edge, and the new yawl intact on her side further up the sand. They must get out to the wreck, salvage what they could before she finally broke up. At least they had brought off the small arms. The muskets and cutlasses and Pusser's dirks lay in a pile above the high-water mark, with the powder kegs and bread boxes. He would need to put a guard on them—one of the few reliable men.

Around the dead fire, his officers were stirring. One by one they sat up and stared around them, unbelieving, at the sea and the moaning seals and the desolate mountains that surrounded them. At his side, young George groaned and muttered, desperately clinging with the need of youth to sleep.

Shelvocke shook the sand from his clothes. Other men had been marooned before and had survived to return to civilization. Dampier had rescued the Mosquito Indian William, left ashore here by Watling in 1681. Another buccaneer before him had lived here for five years. And Selkirk, beached by Bully Stradling in Dampier's 1703 expedition, had made so good a living on Mas a Tierra that when Woodes Rogers had found him, he was at first reluctant to leave. If nothing else, George Shelvocke was a survivor. He'd proved that last night, in the rain-lashed, howling dark, and in those wretched years of peace. He had been beached before.

Like most of the crew, he now owned only the clothes he stood in. By his side on the sand was the brass-bound chest containing his commission scroll and eleven hundred silver dollars of the owners' money. The remainder was underwater at the bottom of the bread room, where he had hidden it from the thieves and cutthroats in the ship's company. It was doubtful whether Hughes, Winder, Neale, and Gumley would now see any of it.

The other officers were all awake now. Brookes sat disconsolately next to his brother-in-law Sam Randall. Surgeon Adams had less than his normal cheerful air. Old Dodd, his white hair matted and tangled, stared gaunt-faced toward the sea. He looked crazed and senile. Shelvocke was pleased to see that Blowfield Coldsea had saved his sextant and chronometer: they might well have need of them yet. Already a plan was forming in his mind . . . unfortunately, the surgeon had failed to rescue his medicine chest, which now lay in the deepest part of the hold.

All along the beach the men were shambling out of the shelter of the trees, grumbling and cursing, shivering and hollow-eyed. Sam Randall appeared at the run, a pack of wild dogs at his heels. Shelvocke remembered that Woodes Rogers had talked of an army of feral cats, other relics of ships that had called here.

For food they had eight bags of bread and biscuit, some of them damp, one cask of beef and one of flour. There was more in the wreck, but much of that was probably spoiled. On Shelvocke's instructions the bread and biscuit were divided up, to give each officer and man as close as possible to the normal ration.

When the meager stock of food was gone, they would have to live off the land. There were fish in the waters, fruit on the trees, fresh water in the streams that ran down from the mountains. And old South Sea hands said that seal meat was edible. Here, carpenter Davenport disagreed. He had eaten it on the Dampier expedition and found it foul. There were plenty of dogs and cats, someone said, and "livestock" in the biscuit! Presently Henry, Shelvocke's black servant, brought him a thin slice of bread covered in green mold, and a ship's biscuit hard as teak. He tapped it ritually on a cask, and a whole boat's crew of weevils fell out. He shut his eyes and bolted the hardtack down.

Shelvocke was anxious to visit the wreck. They needed to rescue whatever might be useful for their sojourn on the island, however long that might be.

He was too late. Just as they were finishing breakfast, they saw the dismasted *Speedwell,* battered by roller after foaming roller throughout the night, give a final heave and shudder and slide off the rocks into deeper water. She came to rest again with the sea covering her decks, only her bowsprit and stern lantern visible. Now the fishes would grow fat on the rest of their biscuit and bully. As long as the bulk of the ship had survived, hanging on the rocks, there had been some link, however fanciful, with home and family. Now they were truly castaways.

Shelvocke made a roll call, department by department. There was some comfort in the fact that only one man had been lost in the shipwreck. That left seventy-two men in all, Indians, Negroes, and whites, few enough for the scheme he had in mind. Afterward the men mostly drifted off into the forest, to find whatever they could to fill the empty corners of their stomachs.

Shelvocke took the carpenter aside and confided in him that, the yawl being too small to hold them all, he was thinking of building a vessel to take them off the island. It should be a small barque, just large enough to hold them. Some timber could be salvaged from the wreck, he thought, and they were, after all, surrounded by tall, thick trees. Davenport objected that they lacked the proper tools, many of which he had sold for grog money in Plymouth. Popplestone, the armorer, was more encouraging. He thought he could carry out all the ironwork necessary, and some useful things might well wash ashore from the wreck. When the sea showed some sign of abating, he took the yawl and a few men to see what could be found. Meanwhile Shelvocke, Henry, and young George went exploring to find a spot at which to set up a shelter.

There were very few clearings or level places in the forest, and it seemed impossible to walk more than a few hundred yards without having to climb a hill or traverse a gully. The going was easy through the trees, though, as there was no undergrowth, only ferns in the deepest valleys. Scarlet hummingbirds, lightly dusted with gold, whirred through the branches. They finally found a pleasant piece of ground about half a mile from the sea, between two crystal streams, with timber for building close at hand. If they could salvage canvas from the wreck, they could erect a tent here, or build a shelter of some sort using branches and small trees, covered with the skins of seals.

By the time they returned to the beach, Popplestone had completed his survey of the wreck, and the yawl with the foraging party was returning across the bay. After some heavy labor, they had brought off the armorer's bellows and six spades, which would provide iron, and Popplestone thought he could probably find more. Charcoal should be made for use in his forge. He had also found the top maul, the mallet used to drive home the fid of the topmast. It was small, but it, too, was of iron, more precious to them than gold, just now.

Shelvocke called all hands to dinner. The weather was temporarily fair, and a big fire was built and lit on the beach. Their sole cask of meat was broached and all the contents roasted and eaten, washed down with clear, sweet water from an inland stream. With all hands in better spirits after the meal, Shelvocke, stiffened by Popplestone's enthusiasm, told the men of his plan to build a rescue vessel.

Timber they would bring from the wreck and hew from the great trees they saw all around them, so conveniently close at hand. It would still be a laborious task, but they were British seamen and would surmount all difficulties. Flattered and cajoled, the well-fed men agreed to go to work on the new barque. Shelvocke spurred them on by urging them to remember that the Spaniards were looking for them. If they were found here on the island, they were dead men. But if they could make haste to sea, then they could soon lay themselves alongside a Spanish trader, take her, and resume their search for the gold and silver in the enemy's bulging counting houses and treasure ships.

Those who had been wooding ashore before the ship was lost fetched their axes and went off to cut wood for charcoal. Volunteers manned the yawl and raft and set off for the wreck to recover the bowsprit, from which, Davenport reckoned, he could make the keel for the new vessel.

So one party sweated to hew timbers from the decks and scantlings of the semisubmerged *Speedwell* at low tide. The rest labored to fell the stout, aromatic, blue-blossomed pimento trees and haul the trunks down to the place on the beach in the cover of the trees that Shelvocke and the carpenter had between them chosen. It was the best spot, they agreed, at which to build the new vessel: not too far from the water's edge, but hidden from a ship passing across the mouth of the bay.

It was hard labor for undernourished men. Their solitary cask of beef consumed, the inventive Popplestone made fishhooks, which were tied to lines made from a bale of twisted ribbon driven ashore. But the weather turned bad again, and for some time they could not fish, being forced to kill and eat seal. Few could swallow the sickly sweet flesh, but the entrails were found to be very palatable, and there was a killing. The rest of the kill was left to rot, and soon a ghastly stench arose from the carcasses and blew inland.

The survivors of the killing fled the beach for other parts of the island. With few now available, the sailors could not be so particular and were forced to eat the flesh, which they eventually acquired a taste for, provided it was burned almost to a crisp. The seal entrails were also good bait for catching huge crayfish from the rocks, to be broiled in the embers of the fire in the evenings. Almost everyone except Shelvocke developed a taste for cat meat. Remembering a beloved tabby at home, he could not bring himself to taste it, though many men said that one meal of cat filled the stomach better than four or five of seal or fish. A small dog was trained to catch as many as were wanted by the cooks of the mess.

Whenever the weather moderated, they fished, catching bream, cod, cavalla, conger, pollock, rock, and silver fish, and others they could not name. There were goats on the island, but the packs of wild dogs had driven them up to the highest slopes, where they moved too fast to be caught. Cooking was done in improvised utensils. The pitch ladle and the tops of the ship's coppers were converted into frying pans, and everyone soon grew used to the stink of hot seal oil.

The drawback of a solid fish diet without salt was that it loosened the bowels, though they were able to garnish it with a wild parsley, watercress from the streams, or a sprig of wild sorrel from the forest. The black pepper called *malagita* proved "Wondrous for expelling wind and preventing griping of the guts." The tops of wild turnips helped combat scurvy, as did the "palm cabbages."[1] It was found that if the tough green outer leaves of the island's thirty- to forty-foot palm trees were stripped away, the soft center growth was tender and sweet. This was an uneconomical crop, though, as for every single cabbage, the lazy matelots chopped down the tree. They also found several small plantations of pumpkins, but the hungry sailors ate them all before they could mature. The red palm berries were also edible.

Living quarters were rough and ready, constructed with the boughs of trees and covered with sealskins, some with the remains of *Speedwell*'s sails. Often in the middle watch of the night, sudden gusts of wind would fall on them out of the mountains and rip hide or canvas away, leaving them exposed and shivering on their primitive beds of leaves.

However, on 8 June, a fortnight after *Speedwell* had been wrecked, the blocks for the building of the escape vessel were down, and the bowsprit from the wreck had been laid ready on the beach. At first carpenter Davenport began to work apparently quite willingly to fashion the keel. Then he suddenly swore a loud oath and proclaimed loudly, "I am nobody's slave! I am on a footing with any captain! I shall not strike another stroke!"[2]

Shelvocke recognized Stewart's Levellers' talk. He promised the carpenter a four-pistole piece as soon as the stem and stern posts were in place, and a hundred pieces of eight (twenty-two pounds, ten shillings) when the barque was finished.

The gleam of money set the carpenter to work again to transform the *Speedwell*'s old bowsprit, soaked with the salt of many seas, into the backbone of their lifeboat-barque. She was to be thirty feet long in the keel and sixteen feet in beam, with a seven-foot depth of hold. Chalking her out was a tedious business. Preliminary sketches were made in the hard sand above high-water mark with the point of a dirk. The wind blew these away, and the final working drawing was made on the ship's old fore-topsail in charcoal.

Shelvocke had warned the men that building the vessel would mean hard labor, and so it proved, even with two watches, each working on alternate days. Making the longitudinals, stringers, and above all the curved frames running athwartships was so difficult that, at times, it seemed plain impossible. To find trees of the right shape or size, they had to go far from the beach, and, having cut them down, had to drag them up and down steep hills to the building site.

For a short time the work went steadily ahead, and, as the men grew used to the hard effort, they began to thrive on the labor and the diet. The tempo increased. Nevertheless there was grumbling, with mutterings from malcontents like Morphew and Stewart. Shelvocke made himself unpopular with some of his officers by making them turn to with the hands, and he himself pitched in with the rest. He walked and climbed every day, worked hard in the fine, wholesome air, and lost weight steadily. No one went sick, though men blamed a lack of normal strength and vigor on their diet, particularly the absence of bread and salt.

But surgeon Adams thought that "Excessive eating of salt meats at sea is questionless one main cause that our English are so subject to calentures, scarbots and the like contagious diseases above all other nations."[3]

The surly Davenport could hardly complain. With the stem and stern posts in position, he drew the first part of his bounty. And the enthusiastic Popplestone found ways of making everything Davenport asked for in the way of tools, with materials from the wreck or discovered ashore. He made, among other handy articles, a small double-headed mallet, hammers, chisels, files, and gimlets, all of which performed very well, and even a bullet mold. The armorer quickly became the heart and soul of the men's efforts, and most of the encouraging progress made was due to his keenness and energy.

The men showed Shelvocke a reasonable degree of respect, and some would stop work to thank him for giving them this chance of deliverance. He encouraged them with stories of other men in other shipwrecks who had saved themselves in similar circumstances. The sooner they finished the work, the sooner they could sail and capture a Spanish trader . . . there were three of the best ports in Chile within 120 leagues of them, and the traffic was thick and rich. . . .

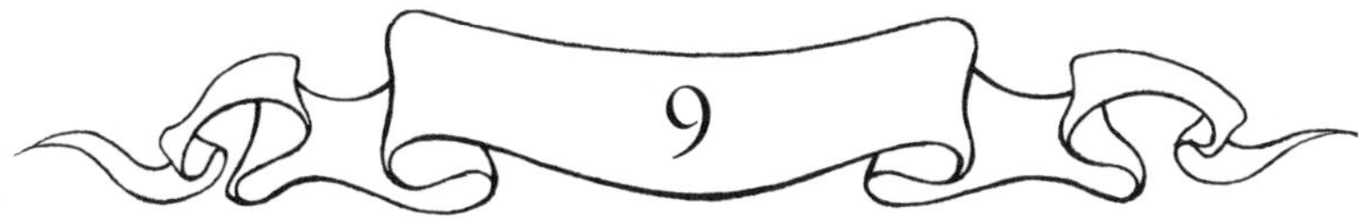

9

Revolution and *Recovery*

As yet, no serpent had really shown itself in this semi-Eden. But Shelvocke was not blind to the groups and cabals that he would come upon, arguing fiercely or brooding over their axes. Sometimes he heard Morphew's or Stewart's or the carpenter's hectoring voice.

Ironically, it was only when the most laborious part of the work had been completed that signs of trouble began to show and the men's efforts started to fall off. Some of the officers, especially Brookes and his brother-in-law Randall, began to avoid Shelvocke and mix only with the men. The first lieutenant had spent most of his naval career on the lower deck and had always been an uneasy member of the wardroom. His manners and language were rough. Many of the hands thought him a good officer because he laughed and joked with them, sought their opinions, and often sided with them against other officers. Others, notably some of the senior hands, saw him as a trimmer and a "Popularity Jack." Shelvocke suspected that he had designs on the captaincy.

One forenoon when a mere dozen hands of the watch reported for work, Shelvocke confronted the first lieutenant, who was skulking in his tent. Shelvocke accused him of encouraging the men to delay work on the barque.

Brookes poured scorn on the vessel, which he called a "bundle of boards." He thought it the wiser course to bide their time on the island until some ship came by and rescued them. He thought that might well be Clipperton, but Shelvocke said that he thought it far more likely to be a Spaniard. In that case their fate would probably be to work as slaves on the enemy's plantations. Their best hope lay in their own efforts to free themselves. Their barque was already half finished, the most punishing labor done . . . Brookes promised evasively to consider what he had said.

That afternoon Shelvocke could find only surgeon Adams, purser Hendry, young George, and old Dodd on the beach. The framework of the half-constructed barque stood forlornly, like a picked carcass. Fearing the hostility of the men, Shelvocke told young George to take his commission and hide it in the woods or among the rocks.

George took the scroll from his father and ran up the sand. He had been gone about half an hour when he returned, running breathlessly toward them, with the alarming news that all the men had gathered by what had come to be known as the Great Tree, arguing and making speeches. Shelvocke at once set off for the meeting place.

As he drew nearer he could hear the familiar tones of Stewart's voice. He left the shade of the woods and elbowed his way through the crowd. No one obstructed him or offered him any insult. Stewart was standing upon a cask, watching him advance. As Shelvocke pushed himself into the front rank of the mob, the chief mate looked straight at him. He said:

> Shelvocke, we have formed a new Association, with articles excluding the Gentlemen Adventurers in England of any part of future gains, divesting you of Captaincy bestowed upon you by them, and regulating ourselves according to Jamaica discipline, with shares for all, according to rank, who have worked and fought in the obtaining of plunder, and who shall have been elected by general vote, and with none for those who stay in England safe and do not soil their hands or give their blood in our enterprise![1]

Shelvocke was promised first refusal of the command on the island, if the majority thought fit. However, he was told, many thought his kind of authority too lofty and arbitrary for a private ship. They thought it more suitable for a man-o'-war, where men were obliged to bear quietly all the hardships imposed upon them, right or wrong, to suffer the press, the lash on their backs for the mere disputing of a command, rancid and rotten food fit only for pigs, and the robbing of honestly gained spoils of war.

A few of the men were not afraid to come out in Shelvocke's support. John Popplestone denied that the captain had ever treated anyone unjustly or severely. Joseph Clutter, able seaman, saw him as rigid but fair. Lieutenant La Porte paid tribute to the skill with which he had already brought them through many trials—the rounding of the Horn in a worn-out ship, beating off a Spanish ship of the line. . . . Their only way home was around the world. Was there any man, the armorer said, more competent to guide them than the captain?

Picking up the cue, La Porte stepped forward, demanding three cheers for Captain Shelvocke. Almost before he had got his words out, Morphew was on him, swinging his big fist and knocking the slender French officer to the ground. Brookes, arms folded, looked impassively down as he lay bleeding from the mouth.

Shelvocke rushed to help the stunned La Porte to his feet. To Brookes he said, "How can you allow a brother officer to be assaulted without lifting a hand in his defence?"[2]

Brought to the test, Shelvocke could not agree to command what was, in his eyes, a lawless gang of Levellers. He was told that he must now, therefore, take his chances as a common sailor.

That night Shelvocke and George, in their tent, heard the trampling and raised voices of a mob coming toward them through the forest. Shelvocke left the tent to meet them. Stewart, at their head, thrust a paper into Shelvocke's hand.

> Whereas the barque *Speedwell* . . . was cast away on the island of Juan Fernandez on May 25th in the year Seventeen Hundred and Twenty, the ship's company thereof are now of consequence at their own disposal, so that their obligations to the Owners and Captain Shelvocke are of no validity, the ship being now no more, and have now framed such articles as are most conducive to their own interest.
>
> First, what money or plate shall hereafter be taken shall be all divided amongst the aforesaid as soon as it can conveniently be done.
>
> Second, in all attacks by sea or land, and in every other such situation, the consent of the people in general is to be asked, everyone to have a single vote, with their Captain to have two.
>
> Captain Shelvocke's share of the plunder to be reduced from 60 to six. . . .

Shelvocke said, "What has been done to you that you impose so much upon me and deprive the Owners and myself of what I consider is our right?"

Stewart said:

> As for the Owners, they cannot possibly have anything to do with us now or require any more service from us. For yourself, you should think yourself well off, since the Jamaica captains are allowed but four shares of plunder, and we have given you two more out of the regard we have for you, and think you favoured in having the refusal of the command of us, which if you think fit to accept, it is well—but we first expect you to sign these articles, otherwise we cannot trust ourselves under your conduct, because we should always be apprehensive that you had sinister intentions upon us.[3]

Shelvocke asked for time to consider the proposition. Inside the tent he said,

> I am distracted at the thought of subjecting myself to the caprices of a giddy mutinous gang of obstinate fellows who are dead to reason and in a fair way of being hardened to all kinds of

> wickedness. . . . But on the whole I think it is necessary to sign the paper. Perhaps they will then turn their thoughts to the work begun. If I refuse, either no-one will get off the island or they will maroon us here, or we might be killed. . . . I cannot call on my officers, who have disowned their ranks and go amongst the men saying "we are not officers now, we are no better than you are now" and will not assume authority until the majority have conferred their former ranks upon them or any other post they think them fitted for—I hear that La Porte, Dodd and Hendry are all to be reduced to midshipmen. . . .[4]

Shelvocke signed the articles, then asked the men to resume work on the barque, which they promised to do. And so was formed the very first seamen's soviet, predating the Nore mutiny by seventy-eight years, the insurrection in the Imperial Russian Fleet at Kronstadt and German High Seas Fleet sailors' councils of 1918 by two centuries.

Next morning Shelvocke went down to the beach, fully expecting to see everyone usefully employed. He found only the carpenter and four hands, who told him that everyone else had retired to the Great Tree. The carpenter informed him that they were all supporters of the new articles and would only work if he paid them.

On the following morning, Shelvocke's tent was surrounded. Morphew and Stewart had come to demand in the name of all the people everything belonging to the Gentlemen owners, particularly 750 pieces of eight in virgin silver and a silver dish weighing seventy-five ounces and worth 250 dollars in money. Shelvocke was warned not to argue or dispute the demand. The plunder came out of the wreck, therefore the owners could have no claim on it, and they meant to have it by one means or another. Shelvocke handed over the silver, and it was divided on the spot.

The men had been told that even the lowest ranks among them were now as good as the captain, who should not be respected any more than the rest. When he was not given a share of the fish caught and complained, he was told "Go and catch some for yourself!" Henry, his servant, was given only the leavings after Morphew and his friends had filled their stomachs with the best of the catch. Shelvocke ate seal, after a hard day's work on the barque. He went to the beach every day, along with Popplestone and a few hands who followed his example.

All of his former servants except the faithful Henry deserted him. Brookes and Randall, of course, always ate with the men. Then La Porte and Hendry left him, complaining that he could no longer feed them. His faction was reduced to George, old Dodd, and Henry, who killed seal, fished, and brought palm cabbages from the mountains for them.

Shelvocke was now exhausted from the tension of events and the continual hard labor that he undertook on the beach. He began to look for an opportunity of getting away in the yawl. "It would be in the last degree hazardous," he said to young George, "but I am beginning to prefer the dangers of the sea in an open boat to what the ship's company might do to us. They will never rest until they have made themselves entirely their own masters by making away with us."[5]

He fell into a deep depression, expecting the worst. He abandoned the barque and spent much of his time sitting on a balk of timber, staring out to sea. Seeing him there, some of the leaders of the mutiny thought that he had given up the idea of sailing away in the new vessel and was plotting some new scheme for getting control of them again. With the arms in the captain's keeping, reasoned Morphew, what was to prevent him from raising a party and driving them into the mountains, then making his escape in the yawl?

A party led by Morphew entered Shelvocke's tent and removed all the small arms. He watched the men wasting the scarce powder and shot as they blazed away at the island's cats and dogs.

More than two months had gone by since they had been wrecked, and it seemed unlikely, now, that the barque would ever be finished. There were never more than ten hands to be found at work on her, and usually only six or seven. These had to put up with constant abuse from their loafing messmates.

Then, one forenoon when Shelvocke was sitting despairingly in his tent, men came running to tell him that a large ship had been sighted. He rushed to the beach to see for himself and found a mass of men milling about, with no one apparently taking any action at all. Shelvocke stood in front of the unfinished timbers of the barque. By her size and the spread of her canvas, he judged the stranger to be the *Peregrine,* their former adversary. If she had seen any signs of their occupation, they were lost.

He swiftly detailed off some men to fetch the arms on the double. Others he told to put out all fires and confine all the Negroes and Indians, in case the vessel became becalmed and they were tempted to swim out to her. They followed his orders without demur.

Anxiously they all watched the ship as she crossed the mouth of the bay. She had the wind on her quarter, and bore away from the island. Friend or foe, she was gone. Shelvocke was well pleased to see the men obey his orders. Striking while the iron was hot, he urged them to recommence work on the barque.

Next day the men met to debate whether or not the work should be continued. This time they gathered before Shelvocke's tent, and he was present from the start. Some men, with Brookes and Morphew as their spokesmen, thought the new vessel would never be fit for sea. In her unfinished state, she could betray their presence. They were for burning her and building two big shallops, in places hidden from seaward view.

Shelvocke dismissed this emphatically as an impractical scheme. Their tools were almost worn out and their materials almost gone.

All the previous hard work would have been wasted, and they would be unable to finish the shallops. Even if they did, the Southern Ocean was no place for a craft of that size. There were murmurs of agreement all around, and the assembly dispersed to discuss the situation among themselves. That there was growing support for Shelvocke's view was proved by a message brought to his tent that night from the carpenter, to say that if work was to be resumed on the barque, he would insist on having his hundred pieces of eight, the money promised to him on completion of the vessel, in advance.

Three separate factions now developed among the men. Morphew's and Brookes's boat-burning party had lost some credibility, as Shelvocke's opinion gained ground. And there had emerged a third party, some dozen men who proposed to remain on the island and fend for themselves. Some of these made a bungled attempt to steal arms from the common store.

These splits weakened the power of the whole dissident body of men. More and more of them began to listen to Shelvocke. He worked steadily on creating a mood for work among them.

Then Brookes came to Shelvocke's tent and obsequiously asked if he might eat with him again. Shelvocke tolerated him, knowing that although the first lieutenant continued to consult Stewart and Morphew, it might help to get the barque finished.

Work with a full watch did, at last, begin. Then they hit practical snags once more. They found that pieces of the wreck's deck planking were so dry that they could not be bent in fire or water, but split like glass into a shower of keen-edged shards. But, thanks mainly to armorer Popplestone's ingenuity, and in particular to the use of overlapping flat planks, clinker-style, to form the bottom, they put together a craft the like of which none of them had ever seen.

Brookes was the only trained diver in the ship's company, and

Shelvocke asked him to go down and recover anything he could that might be useful on the voyage from the wreck. Rigging block and tackle, he brought up one small cannon.

Old rope from the *Speedwell* was remade, her canvas patched up for sails. Masts were rigged. Caulking was a problem, with their worn, improvised tools and lack of proper materials. On the first dry-land test, water that was poured into the boat trickled out immediately through the seams, and a cry arose: "A sieve! A sieve!"[6] Brookes recovered the old ship's pumps. They were badly smashed, but the unfazable Popplestone repaired them and managed to fit them to the new vessel.

Provisions were even more difficult. There were about six bushels of flour left, which would not go very far. They experimented with the curing of fish and seal, but without salt it seemed impossible. Then someone hit on a way of preserving conger eels by splitting them, taking out the backbones, dipping them in salt water, and hanging them up to dry in thick smoke. It would not work with any other fish. Popplestone made more hooks for fishing. To supplement the yawl, small coracles were made of branches and sealskin, and at least two hundred eels a day were brought in. Strict watch was kept on the boats at night. The cooper made casks for water.

It was decided to launch the new barque on the next spring tide, 5 October. There were many doubters. "She will never float. . . . Her seams will open. . . . She will never manage on the open sea. . . ."[7]

The moment came. All hands heaved to send her down the ways. She moved about halfway down toward the water, then the aftermost blocks gave way beneath her, and she canted over and stuck in the sand. But purchases were rigged, and she was hauled upright again. This time she made the water and floated clear. There was a cheer, and Shelvocke named her *Recovery.*

He knew that it was dangerous to let the new vessel lie very long in the bay, with only a big stone for an anchor and a thin rope to hold her. The least puff of wind might drive her on to the rocks, so he urged all hands to store the vessel fast. The water barrels were stowed on the double, and 2,300 smoked eels, along with sixty gallons of seal oil for frying them. One pump proved enough to keep the *Recovery* free of water. The yawl was to be towed behind her.

On 6 October Shelvocke got everyone who wished to leave on board, and the *Recovery,* the Levellers' barque, sailed from Juan Fernandez. Remaining behind were: William Blew, Jacob Boudan, William Coon, Louis Dassort, William Giddy, Joshua Manero, and Edward Osting.

A Resolute Despair

IT WAS like a voyage in hell, forty men and four live hogs crammed into one thirty-foot boat, lying on bundles of smoked eels, their main sustenance, with no way of keeping clean or of exercising. They sucked up stale water from a cask with a musket barrel, the same one for all. The fire for cooking was kept going in a half-tub filled with earth amidships, and there was a continuous noise and stink of frying eels from morning till night, always with violent contention for the frying pan. With only sixteen inches of freeboard, *Recovery* shipped water continually. There was only a grating deck and no awning to put up for protection from the weather, except for a piece of worn, frayed canvas. The pump from *Speedwell* barely kept them dry.

The need to capture a larger vessel was paramount. Shelvocke steered southeast for Concepción, the nearest port, foregoing the easier sailing they could have had by keeping close to the wind, in the interest of getting there as soon as possible.

In the moonlight at four in the morning on 10 October, four days out from Fernandez, they fell in with a large ship that Shelvocke identified plainly as European built. She was bigger and much more heavily gunned than the *Recovery*.

To the Speedwells' surprise the Spaniard wore ship, hoisted colors, fired a gun, hauled close on a wind to westward, and crowded away from them at a great rate of knots. Two hours later the wind died. *Recovery* took to the oars and drew closer to the enemy. Their

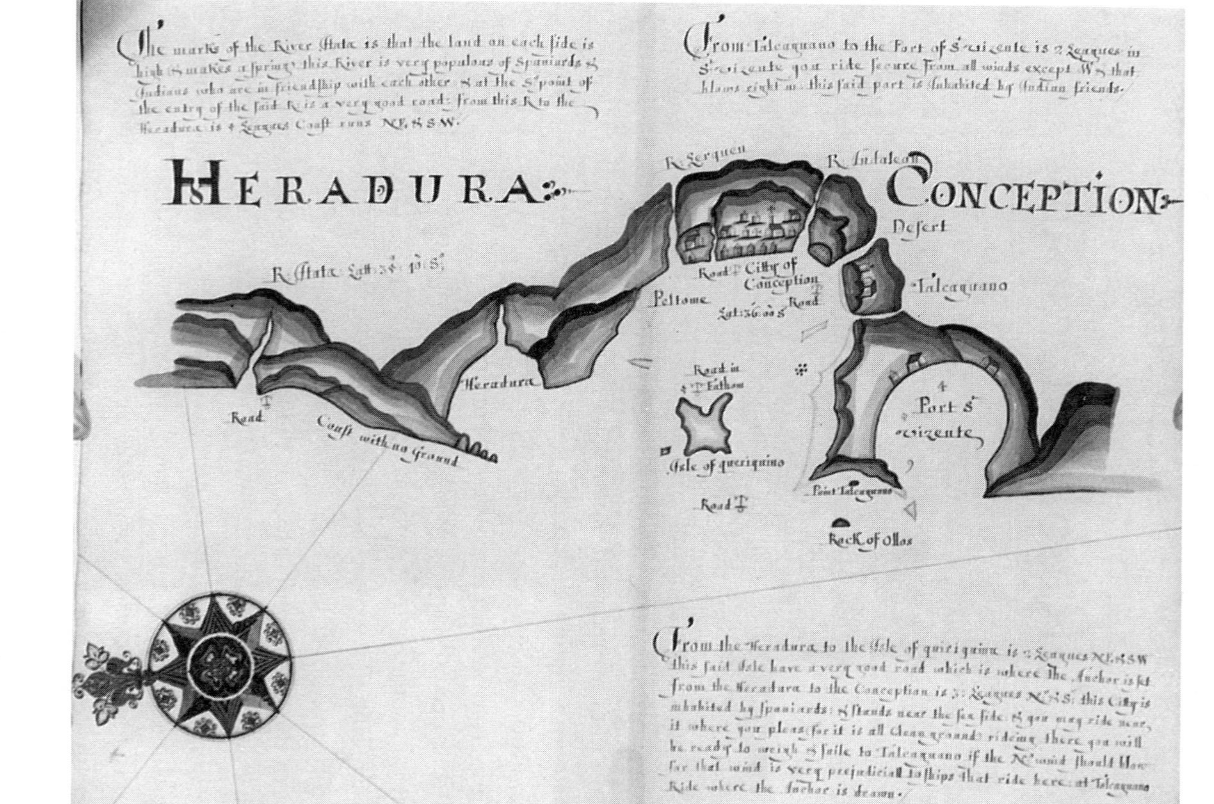

Concepción and Herradura. (Hack, NMM)

situation was so uneven as to be ludicrous. Boarding was their sole means of taking a ship, but a third of their muskets lacked flints, and there were only three cutlasses between them. Their one small cannon could not be properly mounted and had to be fired as it lay on the grating deck, with ammunition limited to two round shot, a few chainbolts and bolt-heads, the clapper from *Speedwell*'s bell, and some bags of beach pebbles to serve as "partridge" (shot made up of scraps of metal and stones, similar to grape).

In four hours they overtook the other ship. The atmosphere was quite euphoric. Everyone was quite certain of taking her, and only sorry that she was not deeper laden. But as they drew near, Shelvocke saw her guns and *pateraroes* (the small cannon used for partridge) and the men massed on her decks, their arms glittering in the sun. She was in fact the *Margarita,* two hundred tons, French built and fast, previously a privateer belonging to St. Malo—the ship that *Speedwell*'s Sprake and other prisoners of the Spaniards had planned to capture—with between eighteen and forty guns.

With as much bravado as he could muster, Shelvocke sang out to his men to stand by their arms for boarding. As his voice rang out, the Spaniards tried to shout him down with loud shouts of, "Perros Ingleses!" (English dogs).[1] They defied the Englishmen to board with a volley of mixed shot, great and small, ball and sharp-edge partridge, which killed gunner Gilbert Henderson and almost brought the foremast down.

Startled, their hopes deflated, the men lay on their oars for a while, then Shelvocke urged them forward again. They rowed up close and fired off all their small shot, then fell back astern while they made some slugs. Three times they attacked without any success, and secretly Shelvocke was glad, picturing the butchery that would undoubtedly occur if they reached the towering deck. Three men had been wounded by Spanish shot: Brookes through the thigh, a foremast-man in the small of the back, Coldsea in the groin. The first two recovered quickly, thanks to a special preparation made up by surgeon Adams from seal oil, but Coldsea was in pain for the best part of ten months.

It was a calm night, though occasionally a faint breeze would waft the spanish ship away from them. Thereupon *Recovery* streamed the oars again and made up the loss in the next calm. Working hard through the small hours produced a fair number of slugs, and Shelvocke thought that they must either make one more effort to take the enemy or surrender.

He put twenty men into the yawl, which they were towing, to lay her athwart the enemy, while he boarded her from the barque. They cast off and were rowing hard for the Spaniard's bows when a sudden gale blew up and drove them off.

As the wind increased, Shelvocke expected the enemy every moment to run them down, which she could easily have done. But the big vessel held north, which Shelvocke thought was probably a feint, with the real objective Valparaiso, the nearest port, to alarm the coast. He steered all night for the harbor, hoping to catch the enemy in the morning, becalmed under the lee of the land. At daylight he saw her, between them and the coast. On recognizing the tan sails of her small pursuer, the Spaniard turned north again and was soon out of sight. Her direction this time suggested Coquimbo, which was better for *Recovery,* as it was smaller and weaker than the Chilean capital.

Shelvocke set course for the new landfall. But on the morning set for entering the harbor, a hard gale rose and blew for four days, forcing them to scud under bare poles, with the yawl in tow on a very short length of rope. With every plunge into a trough, there was the danger of the boat overtaking *Recovery* and smashing into her stern, especially on one great hollow sea that looked as if it was about to pick up the yawl and deposit it right aboard the barque. The men were wet, starved, miserable, and hopeless, and many of them swore to get ashore as soon as possible and stay there.

Then Shelvocke thought of Iquique, the guano island mentioned in Frezier's book as offering good holding ground. Just then the sun came out, "the western wave was all a-flame,"[2] and they made for this sanctuary, passing a small island called Pavilion because it resembled a tent.

Next evening they sighted Iquique, a totally white rock at the foot of the high land of Casapucho. With no anchor, *Recovery* was forced to keep the sea. There was no ship there, and the crew thought it must be the wrong place, some uninhabited spot. Then they heard the barking of dogs and saw the flickering of candlelight. They made the boats fast to a thick float of seaweed until daybreak, when they rowed in between the rocks and were greeted by a group of Indians. They went to the house of the lieutenant commanding Iquique, found it locked, broke in, and looted it and the whole village. They found booty that was far more welcome to them at this point than gold or silver: 60 bushels of wheat flour, 120 calavances and corn, some jerked beef, pork and mutton, a large amount of well-cured fish, many fowls, some rusk, four or five days' eating of soft white bread, six jars of Peruvian wine and brandy, and a large boat on the beach to help them carry off their plunder, though it was a hard struggle for the yawl to tow the other overloaded boat through the great tumbling swell.

Meanwhile the barque had been carried away to the north by the current, out of sight of the island. Shelvocke was afraid that the yawl had deserted them or been sunk. Then he saw the two boats approaching them, loaded down to the gunwales. Famine now changed to plenty, amid universal joy. Shelvocke rationed the wine to half a pint per man per day. After a day or two on their new, wholesome diet, they wondered how even the cast-iron stomachs of English tars could have digested the rank, nauseous eels fried in train oil.

The island of Iquique had an all-white appearance because it seemed to consist entirely of cormorants' dung, called guano, the same that made the rocky coast of Chile look like the blessed White Cliffs of Dover. The stench was incredible. In fact, the *Recovery* could probably have steered for the island entirely by the smell.

Warned of a warship lying off Arica, they steered well clear of it and headed south for the roadsteads of La Nasco and Pisco, both noted for the exports of wine and brandy. As they approached the sierra of La Nasco two hours before daylight, they met a large ship. The action that followed was almost a repeat of the *Margarita* affair, including periods of dead calm. For seven hours they struggled hard to overtake her. The enemy lightened ship by throwing overboard a deck cargo of lumber, and *Recovery* was forced to abandon the chase when a strong breeze blew in too high for the little barque to trap it in her sails. She would almost certainly have been smashed to pieces against the enemy's side if boarding had been attempted.

This ship was the *San Francisco Palacio,* seven hundred tons, eight guns, ten *pateraroes,* plenty of small arms, and a big crew. She was so deep-loaded that as she rolled, the water swilled in through her scuppers and over the upper deck. She had a steep waist accentuated by the height of her fore and poop castles, in the Malaga style.

There were only twenty small arms in *Recovery,* and her men despaired of taking anything in their present condition. Indeed, many of them wanted to surrender to the Spaniard, which lay all night becalmed near them. Shelvocke put, as he thought, two trustworthy men in each boat to prevent this, but the two in the yawl took off in her. Shelvocke feared being reported at Callao, now very close, in a day or two. Next day he was told that Brookes and Morphew had got up a party, too strong for Shelvocke to oppose, to take the remaining boat. But the wind blew fresh, and they could not carry it out.

Next day they stood into the roadstead of Pisco, where they found another large ship. Shelvocke took Brookes aside, told him that his plot was known, and appealed to him for support in this last effort to preserve their liberty. The first lieutenant agreed, and Shelvocke ordered everyone to prepare for boarding immediately.

"This being agreed on," says Shelvocke, "we bore down to her with a resolute despair, and laid athwart the hawse, and to my great satisfaction were received (instead of resistance) by the Captain and all his officers with their hats off, in the most submissive manner, asking for quarter."[3]

She was the good ship *Jesu Maria,* two hundred tons, laden with pitch, tar, copper, and plank. The Spanish captain offered sixteen thousand dollars for her ransom, but this time Shelvocke had other plans. Now they could leave their little *Recovery,* the masts of which had been disabled in boarding in any case, and enjoy themselves in the space and cleanliness of a real ship.

The little homemade barque had done her job, and done it well. They took out of her everything useful and moved into the *Jesu Maria,* which smelled of pitch, but that was preferable to the stink of frying conger eels. The Spanish captain told them that the *Margarita* had arrived at Callao at the same time as the *Jesu Maria* and had given him a full account of the fight with the English barque, in which the Spanish captain and three of his men had been killed, the priest and several others wounded. But with an additional ten guns and fifty men, she was now ready to put to sea again to search for the *Recovery.* The *Flying Fish,* a frigate of twenty-eight guns that *Speedwell* prisoners had helped to fit out, was already on that errand, with the whole coast alerted to catch them.

Guns were firing from the town all night to warn them off landing, and Shelvocke, in the jaws of his enemies, meant to sail as soon as possible before he could be caught here and shot to pieces.

He presented the *Recovery* to the Spanish captain, weighed as soon as the breeze sprang up, and, when reaching for a safe offing from the hostile coast, overhauled his stolen boat. The two thieves were drowsy and delirious. With no food or water for three days, they had just been ashore on a small island near the harbor to kill some seals and drink their blood.

Shelvocke kept the *Jesu Maria* close-hauled until she had gained a two-degree offing. He held her at that until well to the north of Callao, then hauled in a little for the land just south of Truxillo. He looked into the roadsteads of Guanchaco, Malabriga, and Cheripe, but there were no ships to be seen. Passing between the island of Lobos de Tierra and the mainland on the evening of 25 November, near the Saddle of Payta, Shelvocke thought that although his force had been drastically reduced since its last visit to the town, in the *Jesu Maria* he might be able to take it by surprise. News of the ship's capture would not yet have reached it. His first attempt to enter the cove was frustrated by a flat calm, then a rising wind almost put him on the rocks. He decided to defer the attack until the next morning.

In the morning the wind blew fresh off the land, and tacking against it into the cove was tiresome and tedious. But once inside, they saw a small ship. Meanwhile, seeing the struggle of a Spanish-built ship to get in to windward, the governor sent out a large boat full of men to help her and pick up the latest news.

Shelvocke ordered everyone below except those who could pass as Spanish by complexion and dress, and more men armed with muskets to hide behind the gunwale, ready to jump up and order all the Spaniards out of the boat and into the *Jesu Maria* as soon as they made fast alongside. The plan worked very well, and Shelvocke was able to grill the shocked well-wishers on the state of affairs in town. Then he continued into the cove, still using the Spanish flag as extra cover, and anchored.

He sent Brookes away with both boats and twenty-four men, with only the oarsmen visible from shore, the rest lying with their arms on the bottom. The inhabitants were taken by surprise, but many escaped into the hills.

Brookes's haul consisted mainly of four bales of coarse cloth, about five hundredweight of dried tole, or dogfish, and some bread and sweetmeats. Shelvocke captured another small vessel that came in about eight o'clock in the evening and, incautiously, sailed within musket range of the *Jesu Maria.* She had only fifty jars of Peruvian wine aboard, and her master said that he had sailed to Callao in defiance of the orders that only ships in some strength were to put to sea until the English pirates had been taken. It was next to impossible to get off the coast, he claimed. It was from him that Shelvocke learned of Hatley's and Betagh's capture and that *Speedwell* had killed and wounded several men in battle with the *Peregrine,* the Spanish captain and his officers having been much criticized for their fumbled handling of the ship.

Men lingering between the outskirts of the town and the woods to see what the English would do, counting only eighteen men in the town, charged down into the streets, shouting and cheering. The English matelots took refuge in the biggest of the churches, but the Spaniards did not press the attack. They marched to the drum in orderly ranks, back to the boats.

Shelvocke left Payta next morning, and the *Jesu Maria* headed for the island of Gorgona in the bay of Panama, constructing en route a wooden cistern big enough to hold ten tons of water. Without this they would have little or no chance of leaving the coast. On 2 December, they came to anchor to leeward of the northernmost point of the island in forty fathoms, less than a quarter of a mile offshore. They drew water from small streams emptying into the sea and cut down wood at the high-water mark. Curious monkeys, iguanas, and bats watched them from their nearby dormitory cave.

Inside forty-eight hours, they had pulled up the hook and left, in a hurry to escape their pursuers.

Having got well off the tracks of the enemy's ships, a ship's council debated the next move. There was a majority vote in favor of sailing for Asia, as capture here on the coast seemed only a matter of time. The ship's name was changed to *Happy Return,* and preparations were made to leave these waters. But winds and currents were against them, and some of those men opposed to the plan sabotaged the new water tank overnight, and most of the water leaked out. This blow, plus contrary winds and dead calms, kept them detained on the coast until almost all their provisions were exhausted.

Woodes Rogers recommended Quibo Island, where the inhabitants lived in great plenty. On 13 January 1721, the *Happy Return* dropped her hook between the northeastern point of Quibo and

The *Jesu Maria/Happy Return.* (MoD)

the island of Quivetta, in twenty fathoms over against a sandy bay. The place was certainly commodious for wooding and watering. There was no one to be seen and only three empty huts, which had previously been used by pearl fishers. There were heaps of mother-of-pearl shells lying about.

At first light next day, two large piraguas were sighted rowing hard for Quivetta, one flying Spanish colors. Shelvocke thought at first that they might be a party of the local mulattos, well known for their courage, come to attack him. But they put into a small cove on Quivetta, and Brookes was sent in the yawl to capture them. He took the piraguas and two prisoners, a mulatto and a Negro; the rest fled to the woods. He took all the provisions out of the boats—pork and green, ripe, and dried plantains, which made a tasty flour when ground. There was enough to make the equivalent of a month's supply of bread. The mulatto told them of a ship laden with provisions that had sailed past in the night, and of another place where food was plentiful.

As they were leaving Quibo, they were almost forced onto two rocks off the northern point of Quivetta. But at dawn on 20 January, Shelvocke landed by boat on a fine savanna on the island of Sebaco. He was surrounded by a big herd of black cattle, hogs, fowls of all kinds, with dried beef, plantains, and maize available from two friendly Indian farmers. After a wholesome breakfast of hotcake and milk, "a diet we had been long unacquainted with,"[4] says Shelvocke wistfully, they saw the *Happy Return* appear close by, the steering party having been forced to bring her around because of some unfordable streams in between. The farmer selected for them some of his best cattle, which they killed as soon as they were got aboard, there being insufficient water to keep them alive, and made jerked beef.

The *Happy Return* left next morning, decks chockablock with fowls and hogs, and stopped at Quibo for water. Here they gave the two prisoners the largest piragua and let them go, with their gratitude. The entire ship's company then proceeded to get drunk on the captured wine and brandy, which made them aggressive and bloody minded. Looking for a fight, they split into two factions, each of which told Shelvocke that the other party intended to murder him. They urged him to protect himself by killing them first. Shelvocke let them drink freely until all the liquor was used up, after which the schism healed itself.

On the morning of 25 January, *Happy Return* sighted a sail two leagues to leeward, and gave chase. Her quarry was of European build and vaguely familiar. Fearing that she might be one of *Speedwell*'s former pursuers, Shelvocke turned to windward, but in half an hour it fell calm. Soon afterward he saw a boat under oars coming over to the *Happy Return.* When the boat officer hailed him, he was astonished to recognize Davison, first lieutenant of *Success.* Davison was even more surprised at hearing Shelvocke's voice issuing from a very weathered Spanish galleon.

11

"¡Bueno viaje!"

SHELVOCKE HAD actually missed Clipperton in the Cape Verdes by a matter of hours. When the *Speedwell* had reached St. Vincent on 1 April 1719, the *Success* was just over the horizon. She had waited ten days at the island for her consort, then weighed and set course directly for Tierra del Fuego.

She arrived off Cape Virgin Mary, the northernmost point of the entrance to the Straits of Magellan, at noon on 29 May. Contrary to his advice to Shelvocke, which the latter had automatically mistrusted anyway, Clipperton took the Straits route. The *Success* dipped nervously into the Straits next day, and, for the best part of twenty-four hours, fought against fresh gales before anchoring in ten fathoms in a large, deep bay, with Cape Virgin Mary one league north-by-east and the southern point of the entrance, Queen Catherine's foreland (Punta Catalina), five leagues south-sou'west. They weighed next day, 1 June 1719. Following the Straits southward, they reached the Queen Elizabeth Islands in conditions of freezing cold.

Clipperton sent the pinnace ashore for water, but the freshwater stream there was iced over. The boat's crew saw flocks of geese and ducks, which were very shy of them and kept their distance, as did large numbers of Magellanic penguins, though their donkey-like braying could be heard. The *Success*'s surgeon's mate remained ashore all night with a sick man who could not be moved. He died just before dawn, and the surgeon's mate was brought on board almost dead himself with the cold, and suffering from frostbite. The *Success* weighed at ten in the morning and made sail. Having missed St. Catherine's and its bounty, the ship was now seriously short of food, especially fresh fruit and green vegetables to ward off scurvy. And the health of the ship's company was already suffering badly.

They were still fighting gales as 7 June dawned, but that afternoon the seas and winds abated. The ship anchored in forty fathoms of water. The northernmost point of Elizabeth's Island was one league to the southwest, and St. Bartholomew's Island two leagues east-by-south. The yawl was sent ashore to look for greens and had the luck to find a large crop of a sort of wild celery, which made a good salad and greatly refreshed the men.

On 13 June they were still in the Straits, steering semiblind through snow showers, with the ship resembling a ghostly Flying Dutchman. Thankfully they came upon a good watering place amid a wood of fine, tall trees, mostly hazel with some beech, which made good material for spare masts and spars. Next morning, the launch was sent away for water to fill the ship's almost empty casks. Clipperton and the carpenter went with the boat, looking for "a good stick for a mizzen mast," the captain's log recorded. Again they were lucky and found a good tree already felled. They found some wildfowl, and the men gathered mussels and limpets on the rocks, in competition with some black, red-beaked oyster catchers. They ate well on return to the ship, but everyone was by now sorely missing their wine and brandy, lodged in the *Speedwell*'s hold. Scurvy had also now taken hold.

The twentieth, the day chosen for moving on, brought cloudy weather with much sleet and rain. The launch brought off a final load of wood, and at five in the morning, they cleared the hawse, brought the small bower anchor on board, and hoisted in the launch. At eleven o'clock, the pinnace brought rough spars for new mizzen and mizzen-topsail yards and a studding-sail boom, and the *Success* weighed. She investigated a small bay but could find no ground at seventy fathoms and was forced to run to leeward again, with brisk winds veering around the compass from southwest to northwest, becoming fresh and squally. At one o'clock in the afternoon, she anchored in a fine, shingly bottomed bay in fifteen fathoms, with the northernmost point of the ominously named Point Famine five leagues northwest, and the southernmost point of the anchorage four miles south-by-east.

The *Success* weighed again and steered to the southward, through a channel bordered on both sides by tall, upstanding trees, their tops tipped with snow, backed by grand white-capped mountains. There was fresh water to be found in every bay, and strong, continuous flurries of wind. Black-and-white-striped Magellanic penguins swam lithely, streaking away underwater if approached, as did crab-eating sea otters and that breed of duck that had lost the art of flying and used their vestigial stump wings as paddles to skim like hydrofoils over the surface of the water.[1] Some 150 years later they were christened "steamer" ducks, from their suggestion of paddle steamers. In the trees green parakeets chattered, and Megallanic woodpeckers, with their bright orange–tufted heads, kept up a steady tattoo.

For the first time in these waters, they met human inhabitants, in the form of four Indians in a canoe—two men, a woman, and a boy—who paddled out to the *Success* with an offering of wild upland geese and ducks, which they exchanged for knives. They were all short and swarthy, with broad, round faces, low foreheads, short, lank black hair, and only a loincloth for clothing, even in these cold latitudes. Each one had a small streak of bright azure painted around their wrists.

Perhaps with previous experience of jack-tars, they would not allow the woman aboard. Clipperton offered them bread and cheese. They ate this hungrily but refused brandy. All the time the woman in the canoe, which was made of the bark of trees sewn together, kept a small fire going amidships. There were bows and arrows in the boat, and fishing tackle. After two hours the Indians returned ashore, making signs that they would return. Just after they had gone, another sick man, seaman Tom Camfield, died and was buried in the turbulent water of the Straits.

Next day was cloudy. The pinnace went ashore and returned accompanied by the Indian canoe loaded with mussels, which were exchanged for some of the *Success*'s dwindling stock of bread. The weather softened, but the conscientious surgeon's mate was still suffering from the effects of his night ashore. He was forced to have one of his frostbitten toes amputated. Just as the *Success* was weighing, another Indian canoe came alongside. One man came aboard as the ship moved off, with the canoe towed astern. As the ship gathered way the canoe was almost pulled under, and the occupants were forced to let go the tow, leaving the first Indian on board.

At 4:30 next afternoon, the ship anchored to a bottom of fine sand and shells in twenty fathoms, with Prince Rupert Island three miles to the south. Another canoe came alongside. The woman in this craft wore a necklace of small, beautiful shells, wound five or six times around her neck. From a distance, it looked like pearls.

The *Success* weighed again at seven in the morning into a two-knot current, and gales blew for twenty-four hours. At one in the afternoon, she dropped the hook in 31 fathoms on a bottom of small stones and shells, with the tide increasing. It was high water at five in the afternoon, with variable soundings of 27, 10, 45, and 12 fathoms. By four the next morning, the ship was dragging her anchor. The cable was brought to the capstan, but the tide ran strong to leeward. A fresh gale rose, and she picked up speed, so that they were forced to cut away the anchor and half the cable.

Before they could get the sails set, the ship began heading straight for the rocks of Prince Rupert Island. In the nick of time the sails filled and the *Success* ran off, finally anchoring in 14 fathoms.

Winds, driving snow, and rain persisted. In the darkness of the middle watch on 5 July, seaman John Crawford died. At six, the pinnace struggled ashore to lay in more greens for men sick with scurvy. The winds forced Clipperton to lower his fore and main yards, and at three in the afternoon, he moored. Shortly afterward seaman Tom Oldfield was buried, and Will Pridham, the ship's master gunner, died. He was buried ashore at six the following evening, with three volleys of small arms fired over his grave and a piece of strong planking for a headstone. Marine Francis Doyle died two days later, just as the driving snow made the *Success* lower her yards again. The pinnace brought off wild celery and mussels. On 11 July, the ship's basic ration was reduced to one piece of beef or pork per day for each mess of six men. By the seventeenth the ship had been driven back to York Head, where she had lost the anchor. They nearly lost another, with the ship dragging continuously.

That morning, Second Captain Mitchell and Lieutenant Davison sailed in the pinnace for the shore of Tierra del Fuego to the south, to try to locate the entrance to the passage that the French ship *Tartan* was said (by Frezier) to have taken when she passed through into the South Sea in May 1713. They found a passage. It looked dangerously narrow. Their rations were dwindling, and they returned to the ship. On 1 August, Mitchell and three other officers took the pinnace out again, determined, this time, to explore the passage thoroughly. The other boats went wooding and watering. Marine corporal Tom Parry died in the forenoon.

On 5 August Mitchell returned, having found no passage matching the one recommended by Frezier, only a narrow strait that led them into a spacious bay full of ice, with no way through.

They were about to turn back when they at last came upon clear water running northwest.

On 18 August, the *Success* left the Straits of Magellan. Her blunt bows broke into a broad channel. Leaving Cape Pilar, the northernmost point of Desolation Island, to port and the hundred islands of the Queen Adelaide archipelago away to starboard, they entered the South Sea. Steering north-by-west, well clear of the Chilean coast, they headed for Juan Fernandez Island, eleven hundred miles away.

Keeping well out of sight of land, they arrived in Windy (later Cumberland) Bay, Mas a Tierra, on 7 September 1719. This was the last rendezvous arranged with the *Speedwell.* They found no trace of her. She was, in fact, still on passage between St. Catherine's Island and the Horn, a whole ocean away.

Clipperton waited a month at Juan Fernandez for Shelvocke. Before the *Success* weighed, he sent Mitchell ashore to set up a cross and bury at the foot of it a letter for Shelvocke naming another rendezvous, and detailing some recognition signals by which they could identify each other at sea. He had Magee, the ship's surgeon, carve his name in the bark of a big tree near the landing place. Magee added his own name. Then Clipperton changed his mind at the last moment and had his name obliterated, in case Spaniards saw it and it alarmed the coast, where he was well known from previous cruises.

On 9 September three more men died, all of them cursing Shelvocke for making off with their wine and brandy, which might have cheered their languishing spirits. Clipperton cursed him too, but that had become habitual. The jack-tars tortured themselves with visions of foaming pots of Portsmouth Poor John beer. The weather, all this time, was uncertain, with frequent rain squalls, but by 6 October these had moderated, and Clipperton resolved to sail. He first sent the dependable Mitchell ashore to look for deserters in the eastern part of the island. Two of them were recaptured, having lived on cabbage-tree leaves. Fish was salted and four casks of seal meat brought off, and the *Success* weighed, leaving Selkirk's island in the possession of two remaining deserters.

Clipperton held course northward, and on 20 October arrived in a position off Callao, the port for Lima. He had a paper nailed to the mainmast, laying down some local rules for privateers' men. The man who first sighted a sail that became a prize was to have five dollars for every hundred tons of the prize's burden. Every man found drunk or caught in any indecent act with a white or black woman was to be punished according to the nature of his offense. Concealing any captured money above a half-dollar meant forfeiture of all money due for that capture.

They cruised outside gun range of the shore and took several prizes very quickly: on 20 October a small 40-tonner laden with sand and rubbish for manure, two jars of eggs, two of molasses, and two dollars; on the twenty-fifth the 150-ton *St. Vincent,* with wood from Guayaquil; and the 400-ton *Trinity,* from Panama for Lima with many passengers, a ship taken by Woodes Rogers when he had plundered Guayaquil in 1709. On 2 November the 70-ton *Chichly* from Lima for Panama was captured, with the Countess of Laguna on board, plenty of cash, and more than four hundred jars of wine and brandy—a godsend to the enforced teetotalers of the *Success.* Clipperton added a marine officer and a private to the prize crew to protect the countess. The London-built 200-ton pink from Panama taken on 28 November was carrying only wood, but one of her men told Clipperton of two rich ships coming from Lima—and two Spanish men-o'-war of fifty and thirty guns, fitted out especially to hunt the English privateer.

The prizes were too many for the *Success* to handle, and the number of prize crews put aboard them seriously weakened her own crew, already reduced by disease. In the run from the equator, thirty men had died. The rest were in a low condition from sickness and meager, reduced rations, with, until recently, no alcohol to keep them cheerful. It was barely possible to work the *Success.* This was brought home forcibly on 19 November.

Success chased a sail, the *Rosary,* with twelve passengers on board. The *Rosary* lay hove-to. Her captain studied the *Success* through his spyglass and watched her boat drawing close. From the number of men in her, he deduced that she could put only a handful aboard his ship as a prize crew. Before the boat could reach him he told his passengers to hide in the hold, under the direction of the bosun, and be ready to seize any Englishmen who entered in search of plunder. Lieutenant Sergeantson came aboard with only seven men. He at once ordered everyone he could see on deck, Indians, Negroes, and seamen, into the great cabin, except the captain and the pilot. He put a sentry on the door.

When he thought the prisoners secured, the lieutenant gave orders to hoist topsails and make for the *Success,* and his men began to search the ship. Naturally the first place to look was the hold. As they climbed down into it, the passengers fell upon them, knocking down some of them with billets of wood. The prisoners in the great cabin burst open the door and overpowered the sentry, while the captain came quietly up behind Lieutenant Sergeantson, knocked him unconscious, and ordered all the Englishmen tied up. None had been killed or seriously injured.

Having regained his ship, the Spanish master made for the shore and was so eager to reach it that he ran aground. He set his prisoners free to get ashore, where they were immediately recaptured and sent to Lima. The viceroy of Peru, after hearing the captain's story, ordered a new ship to be built for him at Guayaquil as a reward for public service, and a general tax levied upon the merchants to pay for her.

One of Clipperton's men soon revealed everything he knew of the *Success* and her plans. He mentioned the cross at Juan Fernandez, the written signals for Shelvocke, and the two deserters left behind there. The viceroy immediately sent out a small craft to fetch the men and the buried message. By the time the *Speedwell* called, in the following mid-January, the cross and the message had both been removed.

Into the captured *Chichly,* Clipperton put all the officers' and ship's company's plunder (valued at ten thousand pounds), along with eight guns, thirteen English hands, and Second Captain Mitchell, with orders to head for an island off the coast of Mexico and remain there until the *Success* joined him. But Clipperton could not find the island, and Mitchell was written off as either dead by starvation or murdered by Indians—some *Success* hands swearing that they had seen some of their clothes on natives at Puerto Velas. One cynic judged him to have "gone down with the island." A fine seaman, he was greatly missed, though he and his devious commodore had often disagreed. To save rations, Clipperton released two other prizes and put his prisoners ashore. It was this, he later said, plus Shelvocke rousing the coast, that betrayed the whole expedition.

On 27 November, Clipperton found two ships at anchor in Guanchaco Bay, empty except for some Negroes, bread, and a few jars of water. His demand for ransom was ignored, and he burned them. On 12 December he captured the *Rose,* took some of her ample provisions, and let her go.

On 9 February 1720, they reached Duke of York's Island in the Galapagos, some 520 miles west of the coast of Ecuador. Here they scrubbed and cleaned the ship and gorged themselves on turtle meat. On 21 February, capturing the *Prince Eugene,* with the Marquis de Villa Roche, former president of Panama, on board, was sweet revenge for Clipperton. She was the ship that had been retaken from him on his previous voyage in the South Sea, after which he had been badly treated by the marquis at Panama.

On 26 February a Spanish prisoner died aboard the *Success.* He was given the normal burial at sea, but the shrouded corpse floated. The marquis, knowing the average sailor's superstitious nature, said this portended some alarming accident. He pointed out spitefully that one of the mourners should have cried out "¡Bueno viaje!" (May you have a good voyage) to forestall the curse.

On 8 March the *Success* lost her launch and two men, John Trumbal, her sergeant of marines, and gunner's mate Roger Pengelly, when the boat sank in Puerto Velas. Here Clipperton got wind of a plot by the marquis to overpower the men at the watering place and make off in the boats. On 25 July he retook the *St. Vincent,* captured and released on the previous 28 October, heading, this time, with timber and some welcome coconuts for Lima.

The earlier successes of the voyage had not been repeated, and Clipperton's increasingly harsh and erratic behavior was undermining morale. On 6 September, a plot was discovered to take over the ship and shoot the officers. Ringleader Joseph Maynard, a bosun's mate, and marine corporal James Roch were flogged. The rest were pardoned, but the general feeling of despair over the deteriorating voyage and the failure to meet up with the *Speedwell* persisted.

On 1 November they left three ships with treasure and merchandise behind in the bay of Concepción to chase a fourth, which had been making for the bay and drew near enough to trade insults. Then Clipperton's nerve at the idea of taking on all four failed him, and he abandoned the attack, though each vessel might well have been cut out and dealt with separately. Next day, however, he captured the *Solidad* and her cargo of tobacco, sugar, and cloth. Shortly afterward, three enemy warships of 50, 40, and 26 guns, and French-built for speed, came up over the horizon, and the *Success* fled from them. The Spaniards retook a prize that the *Success* had had with her, but the loss of a sail in the flagship was enough to turn them back.

The *Success*'s bottom was not cleaned often enough, which reduced her speed. Clipperton was several times presented with the time and place to do it. Five ships from Coquimbo outsailed him, and he let slip the *Flying Fish,* the ship searching for the *Mercury* and on her way homeward, laden with a rich cargo for Cadiz.

It was shortly after this, on 25 January 1721, that the *Success* fell in with the *Jesu Maria/Happy Return* and heard the voices of squadron mates given up for lost.

12

Happy Return

BEFORE SHELVOCKE and Clipperton could exchange visits, a gale blew up and separated the ships. Afterward, the *Happy Return* closed the *Success.* Shelvocke went aboard and gave Clipperton and Godfrey, the Gentlemen Adventurers' agent general, an account of his adventures. He expressed the hope that they could now combine, to the greater detriment of the king of Spain.

Clipperton returned his overtures by abusing Shelvocke for losing the *Speedwell* and sneering at the quality of her replacement. He refused to help the *Happy Return* with provisions or medical supplies for her wounded men, as his own men were sickly and on short allowance. An angry Shelvocke returned to the *Happy Return,* having arranged to come back in the morning.

Early in the forenoon, he was being pulled across to the *Success* when she suddenly spread all her canvas and crowded away from him. Shelvocke went back to the *Happy Return,* made distress signals, and fired a gun several times.

Clipperton disregarded all these, until his officers protested at his barbarity in leaving his needy colleague behind, especially when the latter's badly wounded sailing master needed supplies from the *Success*'s medical chest. Clipperton was forced to heave to, and Shelvocke sent Brookes to ask for an explanation of his extraordinary conduct and repeat the request for necessities, which Shelvocke even promised to pay for.

With great reluctance, Clipperton then parted with two quarterdeck guns, sixty round shot, some musket balls and flints, one half-hour and one half-minute glass timer, a compass, three hundredweights of salt, and maps of the coast of Mexico and parts of India and China. But he steadfastly refused anything out of his surgeon's chest for poor Coldsea, who was still suffering painfully from his groin wound acquired in the fight with the *Margarita.* In exchange for these goods, Shelvocke bartered some bales of coarse broadcloth, as much pitch and tar as Clipperton asked for, some pigs of copper, a large silver ladle, and a dozen spades.

When the two men met over this transaction, Shelvocke once again offered to combine with the *Success* for the next operations. The *Happy Return,* he pointed out, might cut a poor figure, but she was a sound ship and could stay with the *Success.* He also had a valuable cargo. But Clipperton swore that if he had a cargo of gold, he wanted nothing further to do with him. He must take care of himself.

Hendry, marine lieutenant Raynor, and old Dodd apparently shared Clipperton's opinion of the *Happy Return.* Weary of the voyage and seeing little prospect that their ship could ever live up to her name, they asked Shelvocke for permission to transfer to the *Success* for a passage to England. Shelvocke consented. They joined the *Success,* which immediately departed.

With the supplies obtained from the grudging Clipperton on board, Shelvocke was for going into the Gulf of Panama to try their luck there. But he was heavily outvoted by the majority, who favored following Clipperton to the Tres Marias for turtle, then stretching across the Pacific to India. Edging to windward, they made for Mexico, but so slowly that they began to run out of rations before they had got the length of Rio Lego, where Shelvocke wanted to try for provisions. But a violent northeasterly gale, which the local people called a *teguantepeque,* drove them past it.

A few days later, they met the *Success* again. Clipperton was now heading for Sonsonnate, where he hoped to receive the ransom for the Marquis de Villa Roche, whose wife was said to be waiting with the money. The *Happy Return* ranged close under *Success*'s stern, and Shelvocke asked politely after Clipperton's and his gentlemen's welfare. But he was snubbed, and the two ships steered divergent courses again.

After this brief encounter, calms, contrary winds, and unknown currents slowed the *Happy Return* down, and they were reduced to a small food allowance. This had to be cut each day, and they would have starved but for some turtles caught on the surface of the sea. Masthead lookouts were mounted around the clock to look out for them, and they were usually sighted by the presence of seabirds perched on their shells. Of course the ship lost the wind in pursuing them, and water and kindling were used up in the preparation of the meat. The line between survival and starvation was still very thin, and Shelvocke proposed plundering some small nearby town. Guatulco was the nearest, but as they stood in for the port at sunrise, a sail was sighted far off to leeward.

Taking a ship was thought to be marginally more of a certainty than sacking a town, and the *Happy Return* altered course toward her. But she turned out to be the *Success* once more. Shelvocke reflected on the irony of the situation. Before, the green wilderness of the Southern Ocean had hidden the commodore's ship—permanently, it had seemed—from their sight. Now they could not escape her, and every meeting rubbed in the threat of Clipperton's sullen enmity.

Shelvocke made the prearranged signal for an encounter at sea between the two, clewing up the main topgallant sail and firing a gun. But Clipperton crowded on sail, so that the slower *Happy Return* would have no hope of catching him, thus leaving her a double loser, as she was now too far to windward for Guatulco. She was also hit by continuous gales, and the allowance was reduced to one small plate of calavance beans per man per twenty-four hours. It was just not enough to keep them alive, and they were forced to resort to a really desperate measure. Soaking and rotting in the bilge were the remains of the old smoked congers of *Recovery* days. Most of the men managed to swallow the nauseating fare, which kept them alive.

In this state of desperation, they met the *Success* yet again. Clipperton's unlucky barque had become their evil doppelgänger, their Flying Dutchman. Near the Port of Angels, the two ships stood so near to each other that men aboard them were able to converse in normal voices, though the two captains did not exchange a word. Clipperton had ordered all his officers to ignore the *Happy Return* as if she did not exist. He was callously indifferent to her wretched state: unseaworthy, wandering a hostile coast, unfit to take any prizes or even to be able to get safely over the vast ocean they had to cross in going to India, for which she had not been fitted out, besides being long overdue for dry dock. Clipperton said to his officers, "If his design is to go to India, the child born the day before will be grey-haired with age before he will arrive there."[1]

It was the venom of a bitter and hopeless man, unable to recoup all his past misfortunes, failing at everything he undertook. Clipperton was a loser.

Even Shelvocke, who had more iron in his soul, was in deep despair, feeling himself surrounded on all sides by threats of approaching disasters and some crushing catastrophe. On 12 March, when they were off the port of Acapulco, toward evening they saw a ship between them and the shore. Shelvocke bore down on her, a European-built ship with Spanish colors flying, swathed in mist, big and powerful. Shelvocke thought she might be the *Peregrine,* which, he had been told, was to carry the Prince of St. Bueno, ex-viceroy of Peru, to this port en route for Spain. But the mist had inflated the stranger's size: it was the *Success.*

The hollow-eyed men of the mischristened *Happy Return* stared at this unwelcome phantom in disbelief. Wearily Shelvocke hauled on a wind, whereupon Clipperton hauled down his Spanish colors and hoisted the English ensign. To Shelvocke's surprise, he made the agreed signal for a meeting. Cynically, Shelvocke reasoned that the cause of this sudden cordiality could only be that the commodore was waiting for the silver-loaded Manila galleon to come out of Acapulco and felt himself too weak to do the job on his own.

Happy Return bore down on the *Success,* and Clipperton sent Cook, his second lieutenant, across in his yawl with a letter for Shelvocke. Sure enough, he was waiting for the Manila ship and wanted the assistance of the Spanish hulk. Shelvocke read the letter to his crew and stressed the great mutual benefits likely to accrue to them all as a result of the attack. All hands expressed their willingness to cooperate with Clipperton, but they insisted that he, in return, must give them written security for their shares of any booty, to be signed by him, Godfrey, and all his officers. Shelvocke went aboard *Success* next morning and proposed a union of their ships' companies for the task.

Shelvocke, Brookes, and Randall were received with civility, and soon a seemingly perfect harmony was achieved. Clipperton drew up the document requested by the *Happy Return*'s men, and it was duly signed. It was considered the best idea to put the greater part of *Happy Return*'s ship's company aboard *Success* as soon as they saw the Manila boat put out of Acapulco, with only Shelvocke himself and a boat's crew left in the former, in case it should be found desirable to use her as a "smoker" to blind the enemy, or a fireship, if they found the going too hard.

It was essential to board the enemy as soon as possible, to avoid the greater weight of her metal and the better capacity of the Spanish-built ship to stand up to a cannonading, especially if built of teak in the Philippines, with a heavy sheathing of *lanang* wood, very resistant to cannon shot. These small balls often embedded themselves in the wood and the heavier ones rebounded, as testified by Woodes Rogers, though this strength had tended to give the Spanish crews a sort of "wooden wall" mentality. Many ships, when attacked, simply lay to, to sit it out until the enemy ran out of ammunition. Some Spanish ships could hand out severe punishment if well fought, and this was becoming more frequent, though poor maintenance and greedy overloading caused some to capsize in heavy weather.

Clipperton assured Shelvocke that he was certain of the date of the Manila galleon's departure, which was always within a day or two after Passion Week, now a fortnight away. Shelvocke thought that if the enemy sailed at night and they missed her, they could sail direct to Guam Island, some 4,750 miles across the wide Pacific.

Guam was the southernmost of the Ladrones (Marianas) Islands, which formed the eastern border of the Philippine Sea, stretching more than fifteen hundred miles across to the Philippine Islands. The Manila ship always stopped there for refreshment. Some three million pesos in registered silver from the Potosi and other mines in Alta Peru, plus another million in the bilges for the private profit of captain, crew, and passengers also ensured that westbound ships were overloaded. But they could thrust their sails into the northeast trades and count on usually fair weather to Guam before navigating the Embocadero, the San Bernardino Strait between Luzon and the Samar Islands, to Manila.

The Spaniards neglected sailing qualities, new sailing techniques, and speed in favor of size and strength. On the eastern passage, typhoons (the *bagviosas*) could divert, if not sink, a monster two-thousand-ton galleon, loaded to the gunwales with bales of Chinese luxury goods—if she had not already wrecked herself on the reefs or rocks of the Embocadero. Nine months after the *San Juan* sailed from Cavite, near Manila, she was sighted off Acapulco with no one on board but emaciated corpses, dead from scurvy or starvation.

Shelvocke was optimistic and thought that the chances of success were good, if the plan was prosecuted with determination. He thought that the authentic lines of the *Happy Return* could enable her to close the Spaniard unopposed until it was too late, and the *Success* had twenty-four guns on one broadside. Before embarking for the *Happy Return,* however, he reminded Clipperton of his dire shortage of provisions and water. Clipperton said expansively that he had eighty tons of water, and he promised to let his consort have as much as he wanted and anything else they might need.

Shelvocke returned to his ship to enjoy, for once, the proper benefits of command. Everyone was well satisfied with the prospects before them, except Morphew, vengeful and vicious, prime troublemaker who, now that Shelvocke had the commodore to back his authority, feared Shelvocke's reprisals for his past misconduct. He insinuated himself into the good graces of Clipperton and his officers, and he transferred to the *Success* on the evening of 14 March. But Raynor came back aboard the *Happy Return* to visit his old shipmates. He stayed all night and remained on board to fill the post of captain of marines, vacant since the loss of Betagh. Shelvocke appreciated the exchange. He reminded Clipperton once more of his lack of water, and once more the commodore promised a delivery.

Thus they cruised together, united and in good order, and with a certain degree of hope. But on 15 March Clipperton sent a boat across to the *Happy Return* with a message to Shelvocke promising that if he and his crew would refund all the money shared among themselves in dereliction of their articles with the owners, and agree to put it in a joint stock, all misdemeanors would be forgotten. Both ships' companies could then unite and proceed to cruise for the Acapulco ship.

Not surprisingly, he received no answer from Shelvocke either that day or the next, and he started to worry that the Acapulco ship had, after all, already sailed. The two ships had established the practice of cruising offshore, outside the range of discovery from land but in such a position as to make it impossible for any ship to leave harbor without being seen by them. As the *Happy Return* was not a happy sailer and inferior to *Success* on a wind, Clipperton would shorten sail to enable her to keep up, especially at night, and he showed lights on all necessary occasions.

In the dusk this evening, however, he stretched ahead of them by some two leagues, not lowering so much as a topgallant sail. Shelvocke was startled but kept standing after him in the night, until they were almost in the breakers ashore. Then they had to stand out to sea again, and next morning, there was no sign of the *Success.* Clipperton had deserted them, without water and far from any watering place. They had no choice left but either to beat up north 220 leagues against the wind to make the Tres Marias, or to bear away a much farther distance, for the Gulf of Amapala on this coast, or the island of Cocos.

Shelvocke kept his cruising station for three days, thinking that bad lookouts were perhaps to blame for the rupture. The crew, in spite of the absence of Morphew, reverted to their Levellers' "little republic" and demanded that Shelvocke sail for the nearest fresh water, whatever the outcome. And it was certainly true that, with only three buttsful for forty men, water was a priority. So they began a run of three hundred leagues on a coast subject to long calms, variable winds, and uncertain currents.

At dusk on the day of infamy, 17 March 1721, Clipperton had assembled all his officers and told them of his intention of quitting the station clandestinely, and leaving the coast altogether. Used though they all were to the commodore's vacillations, they were aghast. What he proposed was an act of extreme cowardice, or of neurotic fear. They had for some time suspected the state of Clipperton's mind, from his go-stop-go behavior, his grandiose boasts followed by paralysis in the face of action, his unwillingness to take even minor risks, his drinking bouts leading to outrageous behavior to his subordinates, his pettiness, and his waspish spite. They begged him to defer his plan, at least until the next evening, so that the promised water could be put aboard the *Happy Return.*

Clipperton sneered. Shelvocke's fate meant nothing to him. If the Spaniards captured Shelvocke, they could burn him at the stake, and he would shed no tears for the man who had been avoiding him since they had parted in the storm in the Atlantic. He ordered all lights hooded and tacked directly away from the coast. The fabled fighting power of the Manila galleons had frozen his will. He took council of his fears, thus throwing away the best chance any English sailor had ever had of taking the fabulous treasure ship. This one was called the *Santo Cristo,* with some forty brass guns. She was extremely rich. One week after *Success* had left the station, she sailed. Gone forever was their golden opportunity of taking the richest of treasure ships.

13

Sacra Familia

THE SPEEDWELLS plunged deep into a sea of despair, having had hopes raised so high. Expectations had made them cut even deeper into their allowance. But, resilient as ever, Shelvocke the survivor saw that "nothing now remained but to apply all our thoughts on returning back again, let the event be what it would; and having reduced ourselves to a very small allowance, we turned our head to the south-eastward."[1]

Now fortune seemed to relent. Favorable gales carried them forward, and, in the evening of 30 March, they sighted the roadstead of Sonsonnate, with the dying sun glittering on the sides of a ship. In the moonlight, Brookes' crew took the yawl in to size her up. Two hours later he returned, to report a large vessel with at least one tier of guns.

Shelvocke plied in all night, and, at dawn, cleared away for action. In the daylight, the ship did not look so formidable a proposition as his night thoughts had suggested. It was a slow job, working in against the stiff offshore breeze that blew, and the *Happy Return* took the enemy's fire on each tack she made, while the Spaniard was receiving reinforcements by boat from the shore. At each main and fore yardarm and on the bowsprit end, she hoisted a jar of gunpowder with a lighted match at the ready, to let fall on the English ship's decks if she boarded.

At eleven in the morning, with *Happy Return* under fire since dawn, a sea breeze blew in to their support. Shelvocke capitalized on its presence by switching three guns to the engaging side, and, when within less than musket range, fired a broadside. The birthday breeze ran them down fast upon the enemy, and some brisk and accurate musket fire from *Happy Return's* marines shattered the powder jars before they boarded. No sooner were the feet of the first boarders on the enemy's deck than she surrendered.

The prize was a fine ship, the *Sacra Familia,* three hundred tons, with wine and brandy from Callao, fifty jars of gunpowder, some rusk, and jerked beef. It was not exactly a rich haul, but she was larger, a better sailer, and better fitted out than the *Happy Return,* and Shelvocke changed ships again.

A merchant among the prisoners made an offer for the *Happy Return* and her cargo of pitch, tar, and copper, and went ashore to raise the money. Shelvocke overhauled the *Sacra Familia*'s rigging and sails, cut up in the fight. He was taken aback when he received a letter from the governor ashore, informing him that a truce had been signed between England and Spain and inviting him to spend a week in port to see and study its terms.[2]

Shelvocke was highly suspicious. With a truce in being, why had the Spaniards gone through with the battle? Why no flag of truce before a shot had been fired? The *Sacra Familia* had lately been in touch with Lima, whence the news of the truce was said to have come. And why did none of the prisoners know of it? If it was true, Shelvocke replied, he would welcome the chance to stay for fifteen days, if water and provisions could be supplied. If not, he would be gone in twenty-four hours.

The governor agreed, and a boat went ashore every morning with a flag of truce. For the first four days the *Sacra Familia* was supplied with eight small jars of water a day. On the fifth day this ration was reduced to five, with one small cow being delivered in the whole of that period.

Two priests brought what was said to be a copy of the truce articles. It was badly scrawled in Spanish, and Shelvocke could not understand it. He asked for a translation, which was promised. Two days later the daily boat's crew, including Brookes, were taken prisoner. In the evening, two men in a small, leaky canoe brought letters from Brookes and the governor. The latter demanded that he give up the *Sacra Familia* and surrender himself, otherwise they would be declared pirates. Brookes' letter urged him not to submit to the governor's bullying.

The governor proposed two ways of returning them to their own countrymen: a march to Vera Cruz, on the Gulf of Mexico, by land, or a trip to Lima by sea. Shelvocke did not fancy a journey overland of thirteen hundred miles through hostile people. The two messengers told him that seaman Fred Mackenzie of his boat's crew had told the governor of Shelvocke's plight and his idea of getting water on the Isle of Tigers in the Gulf of Amapala. The governor had moved to put a stop to that. He thought the Englishman to be in a hopeless situation, and he expected him to surrender.

Shelvocke himself was beginning to think that this was probably inevitable, but he wanted to secure the best terms, which would mean sending another message to the governor. He did not want to entrust this to another member of his crew, who would probably also be taken prisoner. But a man volunteered for the mission. Shelvocke offered to talk terms if allowed a safe conduct to Panama, by way of Porto Bello, to some British plantation. The governor was to signal his agreement to these conditions by firing two guns that night and sending the boat and its crew back, with the usual supply of water.

There was no such reply, and Shelvocke weighed in the *Sacra Familia* just before dawn, lying in the bay until ten in the morning to give the governor a last chance. But there was no sign, so he made sail, drawing up a protest against the conduct of the governor, Don Manuel de Medino Salerzaro. Everyone on board signed it—now only twenty-three men to handle the three-hundred-ton *Sacra Familia* and her heavy cotton sails.

At sea they were now reduced to one pint of water per man every twenty-four hours. Coldsea set course for the Gulf of Amapala, some thirty-five leagues away to the east-sou'east. The seriously reduced complement could not have sailed the ship without the help of the Negro prisoners, who proved to be very able sailors. Shelvocke's main consideration now was getting enough water for the trip to Panama, where they would rest and replenish, if peace really existed between Spain and England.

Favorable winds brought them to the gulf on 10 April, in the evening. There they were among several small islands, including the Isle of Tigers. But there was not a drop of fresh water to be had on any of them, even the greener ones. There was no way back. Sonsonnate would take a month's hard sailing, which was out of the question. They could not surrender to the Indians here, or sail to leeward for Rio Lego without a pilot, not to mention their being too weak to make it.

Time, wrote Shelvocke, had now "reduced us to such extremities as we had never known. . . . Ready to sink under the burden of our calamities, we weighed our anchor on the 13th of April before daybreak." Then, "Having now the open sea before us," he wrote with a note of fresh determination, "I brought my people to an obstinate resolution not, by any means, to surrender on this part of the coast, let the consequences be ever so miserable."[3] To this there was unanimous agreement. With less than forty gallons of fresh water left in the ship, the allowance was again reduced, to half a pint per man every twenty-four hours. Even that was overgenerous when there was no watering, that they knew of, nearer than Quibo.

They shaped course for the island, but the weather turned against them again. Thirteen long days passed on the starvation allowance, in extremes of thirst such that they could not get an ounce of food down. Some men constantly drank their own urine, which moistened their mouths for a time, but only led to increased thirst. Others tried to drink large quantities of sea water, which could have killed them. "An universal fever and languid decay of spirits now reigned amongst us," wrote Shelvocke, "and there was not one of us . . . that was not fitter for to be carried to a sick bed than . . . to manage a large ship in a place subject to sudden violent gusts and squalls of wind, yet . . . we were forced to crowd along with all our sail, to reach the place where we hoped to be rescued from a lingering death."[4]

On 25 April they came up with the island of Cano, which looked green enough to offer water if they could get ashore, and there were some tantalizing heavy clouds overhead that looked swollen with rain but refused to open. The *Sacra Familia* came to anchor off the northwest side of the island. It was as much as the men could do to handle the heavy sails or stop the cable. Shelvocke sent Sam Randall and a canoe in through the boiling surf. Evening came with no sign of them. Then, to Shelvocke's unspeakable satisfaction, they returned with all their jars filled. Even so, there were only sixty to seventy gallons, and rationing was still needed. Shelvocke issued one quart to each man immediately.

Randall said the surf was too dangerous for another attempt right away. But that night there were heavy showers of rain, pennies from heaven to the parched and half-crazy men, who caught what they could in sheets, blankets, and pieces of canvas. The bosun made another attempt next day and circled the island, but he found nowhere to land. Thinking that they had enough water now to last them the thirty leagues to Quibo, Shelvocke weighed next day. But then, near the island they found a smooth beach, and the boat went off again and brought off nine full water jars. Then the ship held her way to the southeast and in a few days reached Quibo, where they anchored in the same place as they had done twice before.

They were now within less than eighty leagues of Panama, where the intention was, once again, to surrender. The ship made slow and easy sail. When they reached those waters they hoped to find some of the South Sea Company's officers to tell them of the real state of affairs in Europe.

They did not know that the company had gone bankrupt a year earlier, when the great "South Sea Bubble" had burst. It had proved impossible to peg indefinitely the price of a stock not covered by assets. First there had been a rush to sell the shares of the worthless spin-off Bubble companies; this spread to the South Sea Company, whose shares plummeted from 1,000 to 135.

The relieved *Sacra Familia* sailors wooded and watered at leisure, exploring the Quibo woods for fruit to check scurvy. Papayas, guavas, cassia, limes, and a small kind of white, sour plum were devoured thirstily. But the unbalanced intake, especially the cassia's lusciousness, brought on a painful purge that lasted for several days. After this the ship sailed for Canal Bueno, the Good Passage, for Panama and surrender. Alligators in the sea near Mariato canceled any thought of landing there.

The usual strong currents, contrary winds, and calms detained them for several days under the shadows of the Guanchaco mountains. On 15 May they captured a small barque, the *Holy Sacrament,* which had mistaken them for Spaniards. The master agreed to pilot them to Panama, though no one on board had heard of any truce. The master also supplied them with some very welcome dried beef, pork, and live hogs. His men were so weak from lack of water that no one could stand at the pumps to stop some bad leaks, so Shelvocke put a small prize crew aboard her and took her in tow. He intended to keep her as a hostage in negotiations with the governor of Panama, with young George as his envoy, as being the one most likely to be returned to him. On 17 May another small vessel ran from them and destroyed herself on rocks in a nearby bay. This behavior made the possibility of an armistice even more dubious, and the *Sacra Familia* was nearly lost on a lee shore in a violent gale from the south-sou'west, the Spaniards' *popagallio.*

On 19 May a sail was sighted ahead, standing along the shore. Shelvocke cast off the *Holy Sacrament* and gave chase. By daybreak on the twentieth, she was within gunshot range. Shelvocke ordered the colors spread, fired a gun to leeward, and had a man on the poop waving a flag of truce. But the enemy fired at them and shouted abuse. Shelvocke held his fire and sent a Spanish prisoner out on the bowsprit end to acquaint them of his intention to surrender at Panama and to ask respect for their white flag as symbolizing the truce.

This overture produced only shouts of "Borrachos!" (drunkards) which for the abstemious Spaniards was one of the worst insults they could offer, and "Perros Ingleses!" and a torrent of lurid threats.[5] Shelvocke turned to unmask a broadside of nine guns. He opened fire, and the enemy sheered off. For the next three hours they were becalmed, with firing continuing at musket range. Then a breeze wafted the *Sacra Familia* closer, the Spanish captain was shot dead, and his officers surrendered the ship.

She was the two-hundred-ton *De Concepción de Recova,* with some eighty men, who had been ready to board until the apparently weak and timid English-manned ship had opened fire. She was laden with flour, sugar, boxes of marmalade, jars of preserved peaches, grapes, and limes, and had been refitted especially to take one of the English privateers, having plenty of small arms. Rigging, masts, and sails had been badly cut up by the *Sacra Familia*'s guns, and the foremast was very insecure. A force of not more than twenty-three enfeebled men had captured nearly four times that number.

The prisoners blamed the dead captain, who had thought the *Sacra Familia* easy game, for their defeat. Among the prisoners was Don Baltazzar de Abarca, Conde de la Rosa, a Spanish nobleman and former governor of Pisco now returning to Spain, and a Captain Morel, once captured by Woodes Rogers. Both expressed pleasant surprise at their humane treatment aboard the enemy ship, and at the small number of their captors, who were all clean-shaven and looked like smooth-cheeked boys to them. A thoughtful Shelvocke cautioned his "boys" to keep a close watch on the hairy Spaniards, who outnumbered them so heavily.

They were now within thirty leagues of Panama and in the track of all shipping bound there. Light winds and calms prevented them from joining the captured *Holy Sacrament* until 22 May. But as he bore down on her, Shelvocke felt that there was something wrong with her. Though all her sail was set, all she did was to come to and fall off again, and he could not see anyone on deck. As soon as he came up with her, he sent Randall to check her out. After a short time, the latter came to the rail and shouted, "Sir, there is no soul in her! Her decks and quarters are covered with blood!"[6]

The inference was clear. Five unarmed Spaniards, two of them boys, had somehow managed to outwit and murder four well-armed tars. What had then happened to the missing Spanish killers was a mystery. The men, John Giles, John Emblin, John Williams, and George Chappell, may have been killed while they, perhaps including the watch keeper, had been asleep. There had been no boat on the *Holy Sacrament,* and Shelvocke deduced that the murderers had jumped into the sea on the approach of the *Sacra Familia.* But they would then probably have drowned, so it was more likely that a passing Spanish ship had come up with them and either rescued them or assisted in the attack on the prize crew. Some of the larger bloodstains had been temporarily hidden under bedding and tarpaulins.

The incident spoiled the general satisfaction after the capture of the *De Concepción de Recova.* The men plunged into gloom, with fears that they, now reduced to seventeen regular hands plus a few Negroes, might well suffer the same fate. Shelvocke was worried that the example might give the prisoners from the *Concepción* similar ideas, with odds in their favor. He ordered them all into the larger stern gallery, except Don Baltazzar and other high-ranking officers, who remained in his great cabin. All were closely guarded. The prisoners, in turn, were afraid of reprisals for the massacre in the *Holy Sacrament.* Through a Spanish-speaking English sailor taken in the *Concepción,* Shelvocke reassured them. They promised to bring the killers to justice, if they were still alive.

Shelvocke hauled the *Holy Sacrament* alongside. She was now half full of water, which had spoiled most of her dried beef. Shelvocke took what was left and some live hogs and handed her over to Don Baltazzar. He also put the *Concepción* under Don Baltazzar's command, after taking out of her some provisions of bread, flour, sugar, sweetmeats, and preserved fruits. He later claimed to have put by the same amount for the *Success,* which he expected to find at the Tres Marias, the reason for Clipperton's desertion being then still unknown to him. He also kept the *Concepción*'s launch and her Negroes, to assist in the handling of the *Sacra Familia.* Without them they had little hope of reaching Asia, which had now been restored to the itinerary. Englishmen and Spaniards parted cordially, Shelvocke saluting the Conde de la Rosa with nine guns. Don Baltazzar's two ships then departed for Panama and Shelvocke for the open sea, with Spanish cheers ringing in his ears.

14

Noble Savage

HAD THEY but known, the Spaniards on the coast had no further reason to fear the English ships, with one halfway across the Pacific and the other committed to Asia, though poorly prepared for it in rigging and sails. Before setting course in that direction, the water supply had to be topped up. Quibo was too near for comfort, and the season of the black, squally *vendavals* was approaching. This made it unsafe to trust the *Sacra Familia*'s anchoring tackle among those small islands, with the shifting bottom there. Besides, they were too close to Panama, where Spanish warships were quite likely riding at anchor. Cano seemed the best watering place, in the circumstances.

During the voyage there, the sweetmeats and the marmalade were divided among the messes. One seaman complained that he could not get his knife into one of the boxes of marmalade and wanted it replaced. Shelvocke opened the box and found a cake of virgin silver, specially molded to fit a marmalade box and weighing about two hundred pieces of eight. Five more of these boxes of silver were found among the marmalade. It was a means of defrauding the king of Spain of his fifth share of all silver mined in Peru. Another method, also found in *Concepción*'s cargo, was to mold silver in the shape of bricks, plastering them over with clay and baking them in the sun to look like the real article. Many of these had probably been thrown overboard before the first sample of silver was discovered.

All plunder from the *Concepción* was divided according to the Juan Fernandez articles, with Shelvocke getting no more than six, instead of sixty shares. The ship's soviet would not allow him the money he had laid out at St. Catherine's, more than 100 pounds (5,117 pounds in 1990 currency). But Shelvocke was counting on meeting the *Success* at the Tres Marias or Puerto Seguro. There he would enlist Clipperton's and Godfrey's authority to reinstate his and the owners' claims. The hands began to suspect this when he talked of going to California, which was on latitude 23°06′north, when the track to India lay along the parallel of 13° north. They thought it madness to run so far out of their way to windward, and they complained that in the time it would take to reach Puerto Seguro, they could be off the coast of India. This unnecessary diversion, fighting the winds, would tear their rigging and sails to pieces.

Shelvocke tried bluff. Professing to be knowledgeable about the seasons on both sides of the Pacific Ocean, he convinced them that the monsoons and typhoons on the coasts of China and India would destroy them if they arrived there before the end of October. This gave them the vital opportunity of making repairs and restocking stores. *Sacra Familia*'s bottom was only single-planked in the Spanish style, and, lacking copper sheathing, it should be breamed (to burn off the seaweed and other marine life) as close as possible, to kill the teredo worm. The bottom was already very worm-eaten as it was, and it also needed a good coating of pitch and tallow. And their water tank, which leaked, must be tested, as their lives might well depend on it.

The ship's company, seventeen white hands and six Negroes, agreed with all this. But they demanded that they put into the Gulf of Amapala or Nicoya or some such more southerly place, for water and provisions first. Shelvocke warned them that the defenses of all these places would by now have been strengthened and reinforced and would be too much for a handful of tired and weakened men. Besides, the teredo liked still, muddy water better than the open sea. The westering they would gain in going to California would make up for what they would lose by going so far northward, and a swift passage of forty or fifty days could be expected.

The council had no more answers, and the *Sacra Familia* weighed from Cano and steered northward, aided by favorable gales for forty-eight hours. But the trade wind subsequently obstructed her, blowing constantly from west-nor'west, except in the night, when it veered to northward and sometimes, at the height of the breeze, from west-sou'west and southwest. These winds were eddies of the true trade winds, the course of which was perverted by the obstacles of the high Cordillera.

By trial and error, Shelvocke found their optimum distance from the coast to be between seventy and eighty leagues. There the wind blew consistently from the east-nor'east and northeast, and they were clear of the treacherous strong currents nearer land, as well as of the black *vendavals,* with their torrential rains and sudden vicious squalls.

Dolphins, bonita, albacore, and the rainbow-hued, salmon-like angelfish accompanied them and seemed to give them their blessing. But the fish were followed by booby birds, which used the ship both as resting place and toilet and painted all their yards, tops, and decks, which they fouled as fast as the men could clean them, Shelvocke noted. However, their flesh made a good ragout, and smokers made pipe stems out of their long wing bones.

At the beginning of August they fell in with Cape Corrientes and were swiftly carried to the Tres Marias Islands by a hard gale from the south. They anchored in the lee of the middlemost island, but there was no sign of the *Success* nor any trace of her having been there. A tedious search of all the islands produced no freshwater streams. After three days of this, Shelvocke headed for the Californian coast, which was reached on 11 August.

At daybreak on 13 August, they were nearing Puerto Seguro, which lay right on the Tropic of Cancer and was recognizable by three white rocks that reminded the homesick matelots of the Needles off the Isle of Wight. The storm-tossed *Sacra Familia* entered the bay surrounded by friendly, curious Indians in log canoes. They were also greeted by swarms of yellow locusts.[1]

As soon as the ship anchored, more natives swam out to them from the shore. The locusts swarmed in the rigging, and the sea between the canoes became thick with their bodies. The Indians, men completely naked and women wearing thick grass skirts, were almost as numerous as the locusts, and they explored the ship in scores. The men, all tall, strapping specimens, were painted and adorned. Some wore headbands of red and white silk grass, with tufts of hawk feathers each side; others wore round beads, pieces of mother-of-pearl, or small shells tied in their hair or hanging around their necks, or necklaces of red and black dried berries. Their faces and upper bodies were painted black, with legs and feet daubed red. Their king or chief was only distinguishable by the black hardwood stick he carried, which he presented to Shelvocke as from one boss to another. Shelvocke fed them some of his choicest Peruvian preserves and sweetmeats, with silver spoons to eat them with. All were scrupulously returned after the meal.

Sacra Familia rode in thirteen fathoms and lay open to the sea, moored from east-by-north to southeast-by-south. The wind blew from the west-sou'west to west-by-north, which made this a commodious anchorage. As soon as the ship had dropped her hook, more natives swam out to her. Shelvocke went ashore in the boat to scout for a good watering place, taking the naked king with him and some coarse blue baize and sugar as presents for the women.

Sweet water was found in a small river swirling around green canes, which the locusts did not touch, though they had stripped the trees around the stream. The incessant, voracious ravages of the locusts had stripped the country into the naked appearance of winter, notwithstanding the natural warmth of the climate and the seeming goodness of the soil. Puerto Seguro was very convenient for anyone lying in wait for the Manila ship or for those who wanted to lie concealed for a while when the whole coast had been alarmed.

In contrast to their affection for the white sailors, the Indians showed great contempt for the Negroes, who were, in turn, very much afraid of the tall, muscular, painted men with hair adorned like Spartans, and of their sharp harpoons, with which they performed athletic marvels in the spearing of fish and the killing of predatory pumas or mountain lions. When Sam Randall took the boat in for water, a large party followed him to the watering place, as these noble savages attended all ship-to-shore activities. They did not remain spectators for long, first coming forward to help the few English hands roll the great water casks over the sand in the burning heat and carry logs down to the boat.

As news of the ship's arrival spread around the neighboring countryside, other tribes flocked to see the Englishmen and their Spanish ship. Shelvocke ordered a large copper to be carried ashore and set up on the beach, and he had a Negro cook keep up a regular supply of hasty pudding, made of flour and sugar, for everyone. He fed hundreds of native mouths every day in return for the friendliness and assistance shown to his men, who were already worn out by previous exertions and prone to exhaustion in the heat of the Californian sun.

Shelvocke did not know if California was an island or part of the North American mainland. The Spaniards, grown indolent and spoiled by their easy wealth, had not bothered to explore it. The coast around them was mountainous, barren, and sandy, but the soil at Puerto Seguro was a rich black mold. Shelvocke thought the country probably rich in minerals, though the natives had no utensils or ornaments of metal and seemed ignorant of all the arts. He found that some of the soil contained shimmering dust that looked like gold, but he was dubious of something obtained so easily. Nevertheless, he sifted some out of the soil and put it in a bag. This was subsequently lost; otherwise the Gold Rush might well have started in 1721 rather than in 1845.

As the time came to leave, Shelvocke found himself reluctant to abandon "these unspoiled primitives. There was a natural harmony and affection among them, and they frequently walked hand in hand." Like Crusoe's Man Friday, they seemed endowed with "all the humanity imagineable, and they made some nations (who would give these poor people the epithet of Savages and Barbarians) blush to think that they deserve that appelation more than they."[2] They led careless, unworried lives, desiring nothing but meat and drink, coveting nothing of their neighbors' nor of any stranger's, and they never stole anything from their visitors. In fact, they immediately returned any tool carelessly left ashore.

"They seem to pass their lives," Shelvocke wrote, "in the purest simplicity of the earliest ages of the world, before discord and contention were heard among men."[3] They had not yet been fully exposed to other nations, who would pervert morals and use on them the cruelty that they would learn to imitate. "As yet these Californians may be said to act according to the dictates of Nature, whilst we act contrary to the just remonstrances of our reason."[4] These Indians were forerunners of Jean-Jacques Rousseau's "Noble Savage," the ideal of the great Romantic movement in politics and literature.

Woodes Rogers had taken the orthodox white European view of the native Californians: "They appear to be very idle, and seem to look for no more than a present subsistence."[5] But these people were not lazy; they were merely not used to unremitting labor. They spoke a harsh guttural tongue, but sign language worked very well. For a time Shelvocke thought of taking some of them with

"Noble Savage." (J. Poolman)

him, in the thoughtless manner of previous adventurers, to learn his language and customs and display at home. But he quickly realized, as a humane man, that it would have to be by force and would almost certainly result in great misery for the subjects, the worst possible return for their undemanding friendship.

Their houses would have been thought mean hovels in Europe, and their diet was mostly fish, frequently eaten raw, sometimes baked in sand. Their bark boats consisted of a light wood fastened together with wooden pegs, and from these they showed phenomenal skill in harpooning fish. Often they paddled far out to sea to kill the very largest albacores, which they somehow managed to control without being towed by their quarry.

Shelvocke watched with fascination a dozen of these Homeric fishermen tackle a huge flat fish, probably a manta ray, a good fourteen to fifteen feet broad, thick and supple and with a huge, hideous mouth. It had strayed into the bay. The attack was made mostly from below, with the help of Sam Randall's borrowed dirk. When it had been killed it was cut up into chunks and roasted on the beach, with Shelvocke and his men being given the first helpings.

The Indians also ate a kind of bouillabaisse of deer, fox, and squirrel mixed in a dish, and a sort of bread made from a ground black seed. To drink, they simply walked into the middle of a stream and scooped up the cold, crystal water. This diet helped them, as far as Shelvocke could tell, to live to a healthy old age. Deer sinews went to make bowstrings, and arrows were made from pieces of hollow cane with a wooden head topped with flint, sometimes agate, edges toothed like a saw. With these and their spear/harpoons, they fought pumas.

Shelvocke anticipated great difficulty in getting the Indians off the ship when she was ready to sail. Thanks to their help, the *Sacra Familia*'s business was done in five days. In the forenoon of 18

August, she prepared for departure. As farewell presents, a big consignment of sugar was given to the women, and to the men many knives, old axes, and other iron implements and tools taken off prizes, which were of special use to them, as they had no metal articles of their own. They returned these favors with gifts of bows and arrows, deerskin bags, live foxes and squirrels.

Reluctantly Shelvocke was forced to scare their good friends off. Five guns were fired well clear of any swimmers or canoes, followed by the cracking of unfurled topsails. The noises frightened them, and with the unfurling of sails they looked bereft and shed tears. Many of those on board remained while the anchor was weighed and stowed, and they did not make a move until the ship was well under sail, when they dropped overboard dejectedly. As *Sacra Familia* left Cape St. Lucas, there was a silence and a sadness among the ship's company also. Their brief holiday in Lotus—or Locust—Land was over. Ahead were seven thousand miles in a worn-out ship.

Shelvocke's experience with "these Californians" had influenced him out of all proportion to the length of time spent with them, encouraging the humanity and generosity of spirit for so long suppressed by the harsh selfishness needed for survival. What might well have been several months had been telescoped, thanks to the local help, into five days. Shelvocke did not know whether to be glad of this or sorry, but he was worried that the diversion might have put too much of a strain on already deteriorating rigging and sails, though he did what he could in the way of repair and strengthening with the limited means at his disposal. They had no spare suit of sails, and if hit by a hard gale in the lonely wastes of the Pacific Ocean, they could be in serious trouble.

15

Slow Boat to China

THEIR REFRESHMENT at Puerto Seguro had set them up to the extent that they could face the long haul with renewed confidence. They left Cape St. Lucas on latitude 23°50′ north for Canton, China, the most likely place to find English ships homeward bound.

In August they were halted for three days and nights by the wild westerlies, five to six hundred miles from the nearest land, an unexpected obstacle in this quarter. They dreaded more contrary winds but held to the track of 13° north.

A fortnight after leaving Seguro, practically all the ship's company were painfully afflicted by stomach cramps. This was caused by eating too many sweetmeats on top of the common ration of hasty pudding made with coarse flour and saltwater, and by dried beef partly eaten by cockroaches, ants, and other vermin. They could not afford the wood or water to boil a kettle. Scurvy and fever struck, with no means of prevention or cure.

Sickness increased. Two men died in one day, a carpenter's mate and John Popplestone the ingenious armorer. Several others succumbed shortly afterward, including the carpenter, the gunner, and two of the most useful Negroes. The survivors expected to follow them swiftly. This was the peak of their afflictions, a lonely voyage in a leaking ship with one of her pumps split and useless, and a disabled crew.

The only relief that fate allowed was that of the favorable gales that drove them forward, until, twenty leagues from the Ladrones (Marianas), they met black, dismal weather, with howling winds that careered all around the compass. Only six or seven men were fit to work, and the sick were forced to turn to, if they could, in the cause of sheer survival. Hard gales raised huge, tumbling seas in which the ship labored so much that the knee of her head and the whole beak-head became loose. The bowsprit carried away, dangling amid a mass of twisted stays and seriously interfering with the motion of the ship. There was no way of either repairing it or cutting it adrift. The mainmast had to be left for some time without shrouds, until an effort could be made to unlay some of the best rope cable to make more, the old ones having been knotted and spliced once too often. In Peruvian shipyards, where the *Sacra Familia* had been built, mast support was neglected, with too few and too thin shrouds and stays, though the *Sacra Familia*'s masts themselves were strong and well bedded.

In the midst of all this, Shelvocke himself, who never rested, never seemed to sleep, and had now come to be regarded by the sick matelots as their only leader, was taken violently ill and was not expected to live. There were no medicines and no food that would stay down, not even a tot of grog to cheer the spirit.

Then, early in October, they sighted Guam. The island was green, and it was deeply tempting to run for relief and sustenance there, after such a long nightmare voyage, especially after the main topsail split on the night after sighting the island. But Shelvocke's stubborn common sense told him that though on the point of death himself, he dared not risk entrusting a bunch of Englishmen too weak to defend themselves to the natives there. The battered *Sacra Familia* sailed past.

The ship was now in a very poor condition, with the main beam working and playing with every heel. Though the voyage was shortening, the sickness was on the increase. Ship and sailors were in dire need of harbor, but Formosa was not reached until 3 November, its hills silhouetted against the dying sun. Next day they rounded the island's south cape and passed through the Bashi Channel, avoiding the jagged rocks of Vele Rete and fighting a very strong tide or current. They sighted fires burning ashore, but they were in no condition to take advantage of them. The sick Shelvocke directed their course for Pedro Blanco, a small, rocky island off the China coast.

At daybreak on 6 November 1721, they were approaching the mouth of the Hema Channel south of Hong Kong, in twelve fathoms. The haze on the sea was too strong to see the approaches to Canton or Macao. Shelvocke tried to communicate with the captains of a stream of fishing boats coming out of the channel, but he could not make himself understood. They steered close to land, anchoring every evening, which was a hard chore for men racked by fever. Four days were passed lost in the mist among many islands missing from Shelvocke's charts, some of them heavily fortified.

On the evening of 10 November, they were passing slowly and anxiously through the channel between two of these islands when one fisherman noticed their hesitance and mimed with his cap for them to come to. He climbed on board, and Shelvocke pointed to Macao on his chart. The fisherman shook his head scathingly but agreed, in a mixture of sign language and a few words of English, to pilot them for as many pieces of silver as there were fish in his basket, which amounted to exactly forty. Shelvocke counted out forty dollars in a hat, and the fisherman took them through the channel. At sunset, he brought them to anchor.

The next morning they weighed again, kept the mainland of China close aboard, and at noon were abreast of Pulo Lantoon (Lantan Island), west of Hong Kong. Shelvocke saw two English ships under sail, passing the island of Macao on their way out of

Macao: An English ship exchanges salutes with the Portuguese fort. (MoD)

the river of Canton. On the afternoon of 11 November, they dropped the hook in the roadstead of Macao, the Portuguese settlement near the mouth of the Canton River. Shelvocke, still very sick, sent an officer to the governor with his compliments and a request for a pilot to take them upriver to Canton.

He heard nothing until the next morning, when the ship was visited by a crowd of *Success* people from Macao. They told him that his lack of response to Clipperton's demand that all the prize money Shelvocke and the *Speedwell* crew had pocketed must be refunded, put into a common kitty for proper distribution as a price of letting bygones be bygones, had weakened the commodore's resolve, never of the strongest. "Why should I risk all I have to mend another man's fortune?" he had asked. Coupled with his hatred of Shelvocke and the gloomy conviction that they had missed the Manila boat, this had resulted in his sudden desertion of the *Sacra Familia.* The *Success* had then sailed straight to Guam, where she had been given refreshments and provisions by the friendly governor in exchange for powder and shot.

Clipperton had sent master agent Godfrey and a marine officer ashore to settle accounts, then suddenly weighed to attack a ship of twenty guns from Manila, that had been lying quietly in the roads with them. In approaching the ship, Clipperton ran the *Success* on the rocks within range of the other ship's guns, which began to hammer them. Clipperton's mind plunged into depressive neurosis, and he saw the ship as lost. He drank a bottle of brandy and fell down in a drunken stupor on deck, where he lay snoring as shot from the Spaniard whistled around them. Lieutenant Davison took command and fought the ship well, until he was killed. Second Lieutenant Cook then took over, also put up a good defense, and got the ship afloat again, after forty-eight hours on the rocks.

Clipperton appeared drunk and sleepy, knowing nothing of the hard two-day battle that he had provoked. He tried to take charge again, but the men had had enough of his uncertain leadership. They deposed him and locked him in his cabin, and he sank into the depths of despair. In bad weather Cook took them from Guam to Amoy in China, and there he allotted the dividend, half to the owners, half to the ship's company, who insisted that they sail to Macao, "a Christian port."

Clipperton had good reason to fear that place, and sure enough, the governor remembered the man who had broken jail there once before, after his arrest for deserting Dampier and taking off with a prize. He put Clipperton in jail again, but released him when he produced his commission from the king. All *Success*'s captured goods were sent home to her owners in another of their ships, in spite of Clipperton's desperate efforts to prevent it, though he did manage to sell the *Success* for 1,000 pounds (51,170 pounds today).

At noon on 12 November, a pilot joined the *Sacra Familia,* which weighed and entered the river. They took four days plying up to Wampo, where they found the two English ships *Cadogan* and *Frances,* three French, and one Belgian. Shelvocke anchored and sent an officer with letters to the English captains asking their help and protection against the Chinese customs officers, the notorious Hoppomen.

That evening David Griffiths, one of Shelvocke's men in a hurry to catch an English ship for England, was pursued in a boat by a Hoppoman. Griffiths, drunk and fearing robbery, fired at and killed the customs officer. He escaped to the *Frances,* which was prevented from sailing until she gave him up, and he was sent to Canton in chains. Shelvocke was aboard the *Cadogan* when all this was happening, and it looked for a time as if he was going to be punished for the murder as well. He returned to the *Sacra Familia* to find that all his men had deserted him, leaving young George and four Negroes between him and the aggressive Hoppomen.

He was still sick, but Captains Hill and Nottingham of *Cadogan* and *Frances* came aboard. Astonished at the rotten state of a ship that had crossed the Pacific, they promised him a passage to England—provided he could pay for it in advance. The East India supercargoes, however, who organized passenger transport in their ships, angry that Shelvocke had not consulted them, canceled the offer and ordered the two other captains to fall back five or six miles farther downriver. Shelvocke and young George felt alone, destitute, and helpless.

But the captains of the foreign ships showed them great kindness and intervened to prevent the Chinese from seizing the *Sacra Familia.* They did secure passage home in the *Cadogan,* but not before Shelvocke had paid an exorbitant sum of 6,000 *tahel* (1,950 pounds in 1721; 100,020 pounds today) in port charges, levied according to the size of the vessel, plus a 500-tahel penalty (162 pounds, 10 shillings in 1721; 8,305 pounds today) for being one day late with the payment. This was a total of 6,500 tahel (2,112 pounds, 10 shillings in 1721; 108,325 pounds today), about six times what the *Cadogan* paid, the largest ship there. It was only partially made up for by the sale of the *Sacra Familia,* which fetched 2,000 tahel.

Cadogan sailed toward the end of December 1721. At Batavia Shelvocke, still unable to stand, took an airing in a coach ashore. But he was bothered by the persistent mosquitoes that bred at low tide in the stinking canals there. Warned about pirates in these waters, *Cadogan* joined a Dutch fleet and safely rounded the Cape of Good Hope, for a smooth voyage to England via the island of St. Helena. They made Land's End toward the end of July 1722, met brisk gales in the English Channel, with thick foggy weather, and, in the evening of 30 July anchored under Dungeness. There Shelvocke and other passengers hired a small vessel to take them around to Dover, where they arrived next morning and went straight to London, which they reached on 1 August.

Thus for Shelvocke ended a long, fatiguing voyage of three years, five months, and sixteen days, after sailing considerably more than around the circumference of the earth and having undergone "a great variety of inexpressible troubles and hardships both by land and sea."[1] But he had survived and had saved as many of his men as he could, because George Shelvocke was a survivor.

His "troubles and hardships" were not yet over, however. Clipperton had reached home in the previous June, and, although he had died a few days later, he had told his version of the South Sea venture to Hughes. When Shelvocke arrived, Hughes had him committed to the King's Bench Prison, or "Woodstock Counter."

The owners tried to get him tried in the Admiralty Court for piracy at Cape Frio and other "crimes," but it was ruled that there was insufficient evidence. No one would swear that they had seen the moidores actually taken out of the Portuguese captain's possession, though it was sworn that they left his ship and were brought over to the *Speedwell* by Hatley. An accusation of robbing the king of Spain's subjects after peace had been declared, made by the Spanish ambassador to London, the Marquis de Pozzo Bueno, was on shaky ground, as Shelvocke had at the time been given no real proof of an armistice between Britain and Spain. Hatley had actually reached England about a month before Shelvocke, but he had lost no time in shipping out for Jamaica.

The charge of defrauding the owners, made under common law, was the hardest to refute. But Shelvocke's brother-in-law somehow persuaded the owners, who had already laid out the not inconsiderable sum of 5,400 pounds in solicitors' fees, to drop the charge in the Court of Chancery, and there was a settlement out of court. The only ones who got nothing from the voyage were the widows of men drowned, killed, or destroyed by disease. Two of them had the bad taste to ask the Admiralty for help, but after several appeals got no satisfaction.

Two years later, in 1724, Shelvocke published his *Cruise on the Spaniards with His Majesty's Commission,* and he presented a copy to the Admiralty. His former captain of marines had by then reached England. He read with fury Shelvocke's account of his conduct and published his own version of events, in *A Voyage Round the World . . . relating the true historical facts of the whole affair.*

In what amounts to a shrill, unbalanced diatribe by an Irishman who had kissed the Blarney Stone too many times, Betagh painted Shelvocke as an alternately arrogant and fawning, drunken, gouty monster who manipulated events and subordinates in such an outrageously Machiavellian manner as to strain belief. That Shelvocke, as Betagh alleged, went along with the St. Catherine's articles and the Juan Fernandez agreement because he had himself, through Matt Stewart, engineered them for greater personal gain; that he deliberately put his own officers and men in harm's way for the same reason; that he deliberately wrecked the *Speedwell* so that he could start afresh with no obligations; is all too much to swallow. However, the assertion that Shelvocke came out of the affair much richer than officially declared may well be true.[2]

A few days after Shelvocke had been clapped into the Woodstock Counter, Matt Stewart was picked up at Dover. On him he had an accounts book itemizing the sharing of 23,007 pounds, 15 shillings, and 6 pence between the remainder of Shelvocke's ship's company, with Shelvocke receiving 2,642 pounds, 10 shillings (133,042 pounds today); four officers 1,100 pounds, 17 shillings, and 4 pence (56,287 pounds today) each; and the others their shares proportionate to rank, down to the ship's cook's 220 pounds, 4 shillings, and 2 pence (10,234 pounds today).

But this was only the proceeds from the silver of the *Concepción de Recova.* Betagh stated that Shelvocke had concealed 627 quadruples of gold, worth about 2,340 pounds (117,691 pounds today). There was also his share of the value of the *Sacra Familia*'s cargo, pickings from various prizes taken off the South American coast, and the money for the sale of the *Sacra Familia* at Canton. He had paid the Hoppomen's outrageous charges, but in the end, he still might have made about the 7,000 pounds (358,190 pounds today) of Betagh's estimate. Shelvocke's account of the voyage was very popular. In 1726 it was reissued in expanded form, as *A Voyage Round the World by Way of the Great South Sea.* His royalties must have been considerable.

Unlike the wretched Clipperton, who died a few days after he had reached his family in Galway, Ireland, or poor Sam Randall, who died in the King's Bench Prison, Shelvocke lived, highly respected, until 1742. He died at age sixty-six, at his son's home in Lombard Street, in the City of London. George Junior was at that time secretary of the General Post Office, and he became a Fellow of the Royal Society shortly after his father's death.

Shelvocke Senior was buried at St. Michael's Church, where his tombstone tells us that he was "a gentleman of great abilities in his profession and allowed to have been one of the bravest and most accomplished seamen of his time." Whatever George Shelvocke's weaknesses, whatever his sins, no one, not even Will Betagh, his bête noire, would have denied him that tribute.

IN THE WINTER of 1797, the poets Samuel Taylor Coleridge and William Wordsworth and the latter's sister Dorothy went on a walking tour in Somerset and Devon, which was to be paid for by the fee for a poem that a magazine had commissioned from Coleridge.

As they walked along the Quantocks, a promising theme, based partly on a friend's dream and fired up by Coleridge's opium-boosted imagination, was discussed. Coleridge tried out some experimental stanzas on his two friends.

On the evening of 12 November, they witnessed the meteoric shower known as the Leonids, formed by debris from the comet Temple-Tuttle. This display could be seen annually, when the earth crossed the comet's path. In this particular year, the cloud of cosmic waste was especially dense, with meteors whose trails persisted long enough to produce equally fiery pyrotechnics on the following evening, when they set out on a three-hour walk from Alfoxden to Watchet. That night, by the light of a flickering candle, Coleridge's scratching quill described how

> The upper air burst into life!
> And a hundred fire-flags sheen,
> To and fro they were hurried about!
> And to and fro, and in and out,
> The wan stars danced between.
>
> And the coming wind did roar more loud,
> And the sails did sigh like sedge;
> And the rain poured down from one black cloud;
> The Moon was at its edge.

The starry imagery vividly adorned the verse, but the whole narrative lacked motivation. The poem was a tale of the dire tribulations of an old sailor, an "Ancient Mariner," second cousin to the Flying Dutchman, who put a fevered nightmare into some very uneven verse, having obviously committed some unspeakable sin. What that sin was, however, Coleridge had not got around to inventing.

His hallucinatory magic was not Wordsworth's style. His feet were more firmly on the ground, among the daffodils, but he did contribute some of the few more realistic details that anchored the poem to a firmer bottom.

He had, the future British poet laureate told Coleridge, on his shelves an account by a Capt. George Shelvocke of a voyage to the South Seas some seventy-five years earlier. The participants suffered many horrors and tribulations, some of them thought because of a curse that fell upon their ship after one of them had wantonly shot an albatross as they struggled to round the dreaded Cape Horn.

The poem needed a crime to fit the punishment. Supposing Coleridge's mariner shot one of those ominous birds, thereby invoking an awful curse? This suggestion was adopted, with the more poetic crossbow substituted for Sim Hatley's musket. At first

> . . . all averred, I had killed the bird
> That brought the fog and mist . . .

Later, however, the Ancient Mariner's accursed barque and her crew, like the Speedwells, suffered all the agony of

> Water, water, everywhere,
> Nor any drop to drink . . .

and the many dreadful torments of "The Nightmare Life-in-Death." The Mariner's shipmates hung the murdered bird, one of God's "loved things," around his neck—almost a metaphor for Hatley's subsequent fate. They all perished, and the ship went "down like lead."

Notes

1. Realms of Silver

1. Pepys, *The Diary of Samuel Pepys,* 268.

2. An Andrew Miller who kept a boarding house in Portsmouth, plied his clients with grog, and betrayed them to the pressgang, is identified by some as the origin of the nickname and is thought by many to be one and the same. Less credible candidates for the honor are "Lieutenant Andrew," a particularly successful pressgang officer, and St. Andrew, patron saint of fishermen (and, by extension, sailors).

3. Medieval London, the "square mile," which had become the commercial and banking sector of the great metropolis, was known as the City.

4. Merchants trading with the Arab nations of North Africa, the Barbary Coast, were called Barbary traders.

5. At the commencement of the war, Louis XIV's France controlled the lower Rhine and both sides of the Alps, the Mediterranean, Spain, and much of Italy. The enemy was the ragged coalition of England, with only a small army; Austria, handicapped by rebellion in Hungary; Holland, a trading rival of England; the small German states, notably Prussia and Hanover; and Denmark, menaced by warlike Sweden.

At sea, the Royal Navy held its own. Adm. Sir George Rooke beat the Spanish in Vigo Bay, Adm. John Benbow swept the Spanish Main, Adm. Sir Clowdisley Shovell sealed the French fleet in Toulon. On land, the French drove the Austrians back in Italy and menaced Vienna. Then Portugal joined the alliance (trading wine for English cloth in the process), giving the latter a broad front with Spain, as well as Lisbon harbor, from which Rooke sailed to take Gibraltar. The English John Churchill, later duke of Marlborough, crossed the Rhine with a mixed allied army and crushed the French at Blenheim and Ramillies.

Finally, however, the military stalemate in Spain, political opposition to the war in England, and financial strain brought the war-weary nations together in 1713 to patch up a peace.

6. This was the third Anglo-Dutch war. Allies against Spain in the sixteenth century, the English and Dutch competed as world traders and colonists and fought three bloody wars. The first (1652–54) was confined to the North Sea and English Channel and favored the English. The second (1664–67) ranged between West Africa, New Amsterdam (captured by the English and renamed New York), Norway, and the river Thames, with peace terms favoring Holland. The third conflict (1672–73) in which Dampier's *Royal Prince* took part, featured the hard-fought battles of Sole Bay, Schooneveldt, and the Texel. The result was strategic defeat for the Dutch, who lost their command of the English Channel and the North Sea.

7. The abbreviation HMS prefixed before the name of a ship of the British Navy did not come into general use until 1790. Its earliest use was in 1789, referring to HMS *Phoenix.*

8. Selkirk was born in Largo, Aberdeenshire, the son of a poor Scottish shoemaker. He was something of a religious bigot, and aboard the *Cinque Ports* he soon fell out with the coarse and brutal Thomas "Bully" Stradling. When Stradling took over command of the ship on the death of the captain, Selkirk decided to leave the ship as soon as possible, with the idea of settling on some remote island. This resolve was strengthened by a recurring nightmare of the wrecking of the *Cinque Ports.*

The running quarrel between Selkirk and Stradling worsened. After the *Cinque Ports* had completed a self-refit at the uninhabited Juan Fernandez Island, Selkirk was left ashore there at his own request. With him he took his sea chest with some clothes, a musket with one pound of powder and some balls, a hatchet and some tools, a knife, a pewter kettle, his Bible, a book on navigation and his navigational instruments, and a few pounds of tobacco. Stradling was in the boat that put him ashore. As the boat rowed away, the potential misery of his situation struck Selkirk. Rushing into the water, he begged to be taken back. But Stradling mocked him and rowed on.

9. Rogers, *Life Aboard a British Privateer,* 73.

10. Left alone on the island, Selkirk had pulled himself together. He had found a cave where he could live with some degree of comfort, with two castaway cats to keep rats from gnawing his feet.

Surrounded by dark cottonwood forests, he hunted wild goats in the mountains, which he climbed every day to look for passing ships. He saw various vessels pass the island, but only two anchored offshore. On one of these occasions, doubtful of the ship's nationality, he was spotted on the beach. The ship was Spanish. Selkirk was pursued and shot at, but he hid up a tree.

When he saw Rogers's two ships approaching, he was reasonably hopeful that they were English, and, that night, he lit a big fire. Rogers saw the glow, thought it came from an enemy ship at anchor, and cleared for action. At first light, seeing no other ship, he sent an armed boat ashore. Selkirk ran to the beach, waving a piece of rag on a stick, and directed the boat to a safe landing place. He wore his last shirt, and his thighs and body were covered with animal skins. He wore a goatskin cap and had grown a great beard, the product of four years and four months of isolation. Selkirk conversed haltingly but established his identity and was taken aboard the *Duke.* He was very disturbed to see Dampier, but relieved that his former commodore was not in command. Dampier, probably to disassociate himself from Stradling, actually extolled Selkirk's seamanship. The Scot was made mate in the *Duke,* then given command of the prize *Increase,* which he sailed back to Britain.

When the *Increase,* the other prizes, and Rogers's amassed loot were sold, Selkirk's share was eight hundred pounds (forty thousand today), the foundation of a family fortune. He returned home to Largo. But as he looked out across the gray North sea, he could not settle. He built himself a cave to sleep in and often took solitary boat trips or walked alone to the local beauty spot of Keill's Den. To a visitor he confided that nothing could restore to him the tranquillity of his island.

Selkirk persuaded fifteen-year-old Sophie Bruce, who milked her father's cows in Keill's Den, to run off with him to London. But there he left her to marry a widow some years older than himself. Nevertheless, in his will he left "unto my loving and well beloved friend Sophie of the Pelmel, London, spinster, all and singular my lands, tenements, out-houses, gardens, yards, orchards, situate, lyeing, and being in Largo aforesaid, or in any other place or places whatsoever, during her natural life, and no longer" (Howell, *The Story of Alexander Selkirk*).

In 1719 Daniel Defoe published the novel *Life and Strange Surprising Adventures of Robinson Crusoe,* in which his hero was closely based on Selkirk. Neither London nor his cave in Largo could satisfy Selkirk. After hanging around Liverpool and Bristol—where, some say, Defoe tracked him down—he went back to sea and died there in 1723, the year after Shelvocke returned to England.

11. The War of the English Succession, 1689–97, and the War of the Spanish Succession (see note 5 of this chapter). The former was largely a naval war. In the closely contested battles of Barfleur and La Hogue, the Royal Navy defeated the French Navy's support of an attempt by the deposed Catholic King James II to retrieve the throne of England from the Protestant King William III.

12. Betagh, *A Voyage Round the World,* 9.

13. The *Success* and *Speedwell* were private ships. There were also ships of the same name in the Royal Navy list, both nominally Sixth Rates of twenty guns, launched in 1712 and 1716 respectively. His Majesty's Ship *Speedwell* was converted to a fireship in 1719 and was wrecked on the Dutch coast in 1720. His Majesty's Ship *Success* served for most of the 1720s in Irish waters and was broken up in 1746.

2. Crank and Tender

1. Betagh, *A Voyage Round the World,* 9.
2. Shelvocke, *A Voyage Round the World,* 2.
3. Betagh, *A Voyage Round the World,* 17.
4. Ibid.
5. Ibid.
6. Ibid.
7. Ibid., 17–18.
8. Ibid., 18.
9. Ibid.
10. Ibid., 19–20. Shelvocke, *A Voyage Round the World,* 6.
11. Shelvocke, *A Voyage Round the World,* 7. Betagh, *A Voyage Round the World,* 19–20.
12. Shelvocke, *A Voyage Round the World,* 7.
13. Betagh, *A Voyage Round the World,* 20.
14. Shelvocke, *A Voyage Round the World,* 12.
15. Betagh, *A Voyage Round the World,* 28–29.
16. Ibid., 28–30.

3. Levellers' Talk

1. Shelvocke, *A Voyage Round the World,* 56.

2. Ibid., 31–36.

3. Ibid., 39–40.

4. Commons Journal, reprinted in Clarke Papers, vol. 1, 105, Camden Society, London, 1891.

5. Shelvocke, *A Voyage Round the World,* 42.

6. Betagh, *A Voyage Round the World,* 42.

7. Ibid., 49.

4. The Albatross

1. Shelvocke, *A Voyage Round the World,* 47–48.

2. Pepys, *Memoirs Relating to the State of the Royal Navy,* vol. 4, 37.

3. Shelvocke, *A Voyage Round the World,* 60, 61.

4. Ibid., 63.

5. Ibid., 72–73.

6. Ibid.

5. Capitaine le Breton

1. Betagh, *A Voyage Round the World,* 60.

2. In the eighteenth century, the British army used specialized soldiers in infantry regiments. Armed with grenades, they wore unique tall, pointed caps and were specially selected for their height and brawn. Their appearance was meant to strike fear into the enemy. They were the model for the elite Grenadier Guards, the first infantry regiment in the royal Household Brigade.

3. Shelvocke, *A Voyage Round the World,* 127–28.

4. Betagh, *A Voyage Round the World,* 72.

6. *Mercury*'s War

1. When Selkirk and later the *Speedwell*'s crew lived on Mas a Tierra, the island was uninhabited. Today some five to seven hundred people live on the island, now named Isla Robinson Crusoe. Their main occupation

is lobster fishing. In Bahia Cumberland still lie the remains of the German light cruiser *Dresden,* which survived the battle of the Falklands of 8 December 1914 only to scuttle herself there three months later, when discovered by three British cruisers.

2. Shelvocke, *A Voyage Round the World,* 164.
3. Betagh, *A Voyage Round the World,* 243.

7. Rocks and Roundshot

1. Shelvocke, *A Voyage Round the World,* 205.

8. Jamaica Discipline

1. Shelvocke, *A Voyage Round the World,* 210.
2. Ibid., 214.
3. Ibid., 216.

9. Revolution and *Recovery*

1. Shelvocke, *A Voyage Round the World,* 218–19.
2. Ibid., 221–22.
3. Ibid., 222–24.
4. Ibid., 224–25.
5. Ibid., 230.
6. Ibid., 240.
7. Ibid., 243.

10. A Resolute Despair

1. Shelvocke, *A Voyage Round the World,* 262.
2. Coleridge, *The Rime of the Ancient Mariner,* part 3, verse 7.
3. Shelvocke, *A Voyage Round the World,* 278.
4. Ibid., 288.

11. "¡Bueno viaje!"

1. Magellanic penguins are seen at sea, often close off the coast. Like Rock-hopper penguins they breed from the Falkland Islands, southward to Cape Horn and the islands around Tierra del Fuego. They follow the cold Falkland Current northward, to the latitude of Buenos Aires. Both

species have been seen, though rarely, as far north as two hundred miles from Tierra del Fuego. They can be distinguished by observing the head. In the Rock-hopper, with its red bill, the whole head, sides of the face, chin, and throat are slaty black, and a line of yellow plumes can be seen running back from the bill to above the eye. In the Magellanic penguin, a narrow white band runs along the sides and crown of its slaty gray head and cheeks, and its bill is black. It usually collects in small parties and swims low in the water but holds its head high, with the bill often tilted upward.

12. *Happy Return*

1. Taylor, *Journal,* entry for 2 March 1721.

13. *Sacra Familia*

1. Shelvocke, *A Voyage Round the World,* 324.

2. After crushing losses at sea, Spain had capitulated to the Quadruple Alliance of Great Britain, Austria, France, and Holland in February 1720. The resultant truce was an uneasy one, with Spain feeling unjustly deprived of its Mediterranean possessions. Enmity continued to smoulder, notably in the Spanish American colonies, where the history of attacks by English captains on Spanish trade could not be forgotten.

Communications were such that news of the truce may not have reached Lima before 25 May 1720, the date Shelvocke was wrecked on Juan Fernandez. He was isolated there until 6 October. In several renewed attacks after that, he flew the Spanish flag. The Spaniards would, therefore, have regarded him as another pirate, to be hunted down.

Clipperton did not, apparently, mention a truce when the two men met on 25 January 1721. Shelvocke's professed ignorance of the truce, when informed by the governor of Sonsonnate on 31 March, appears genuine, although both British captains (and, indeed, their masters in London) would, feasibly, have put loot above the law. On the following 15 May, Shelvocke in the *Sacra Familia* captured the barque *Holy Sacrament,* which had taken him for Spanish. No one on board her had heard of any truce.

3. Shelvocke, *A Voyage Round the World,* 350.

4. Ibid., 360.

5. Ibid., 369.

6. Ibid., 374.

14. Noble Savage

1. The bay that the Spaniards had named Puerto Seguro (safe port) would seem to have been located in the territory of the Huchiti tribe, bordered to the north by the much larger Guaycura tribe and to the south, at the tip of the Baja California peninsula, by the Pericu tribe.

2. Shelvocke, *A Voyage Round the World,* 405–6.

3. Ibid., 407.

4. Ibid., 408.

5. Rogers, *A Cruising Voyage Round the World,* 173.

15. Slow Boat to China

1. Shelvocke, *A Voyage Round the World,* 468.

2. It must be said that in the two accounts of his voyage, Shelvocke offers a somewhat idealized self-portrait. Had he not been astute, and, at times, devious and wily, the seamen's soviet formed aboard the *Speedwell* might have ousted him for good, leaving the future for all concerned in infirm hands.

Glossary

Apeak: Anchor at deck or hawse level, ready to let go.

Beak-head: Extreme point of the bows, formerly the bird's beak–like end of an ancient galley's pointed prow, often ornamented, for piercing an enemy vessel's side ("Xerxes' navy with their hostile beaks," William Glover, *Leonidas,* 1738, p. 63). Revived in the ram of nineteenth-century capital ships.

Bully: Boxed or tinned beef.

Burgoo or *burgou:* Porridge.

Caffader meal: Mixture made from husks of corn, or sometimes from peas or beans.

Calenture: Sailors' delirium in the tropics showing them the sea as green fields. From Latin *caleo,* to be hot.

Cassia: A kind of cinnamon.

Cat: Cat-o'-nine-tails. Rope whip with a handle and nine knotted lashes.

Chippy: Slang for a ship's carpenter.

Cod-pepper: Capsicum, or guinea pepper, a tropical plant or shrub with hot, pungent capsules and seeds from which the commercial Chillios was produced, chief ingredient of cayenne pepper. Capsicine, extracted from its capsules, was reported in 1801 as a partial remedy for gangrene.

Crank: Said of a ship liable to heel or roll excessively because of oversparring.

Drummer: Con man or persuader of people out of their money or goods (like the modern American drummer, or traveling salesman). Also called *busker* (in twentieth-century English, a street entertainer).

Eight bells: Time is denoted at sea by striking the ship's bell every half hour—one stroke at half-past four, half-past eight, and half-past twelve, with one more stroke added for each half-hour until eight strokes of the bell, or eight bells, are reached at four, eight, and twelve. The dog watches (4:00 to 6:00 P.M. and 6:00 to 8:00 P.M., or 1600–1800 and 1800–2000) are different: 6:30 P.M. (1830) is one bell, 7:00 P.M. (1900) two bells, and 7:30 P.M. (1930) three bells. But 8:00 P.M. (2000) is always eight bells.

Fid (fidder): A square-sectioned bar of wood or iron with a shoulder at one end, used to support the weight of a topmast and also a topgallant mast. Formerly *fidd.* It is knocked home with a fid hammer (or maul). The term is also applied to a nine- to thirty-inch conical pin of hardwood used to open the strands of a rope in splicing. A fid hammer could also be a dual-purpose fid, sharp at one end for splicing, hammer-shaped at the other for fidding. The term later came to mean several different things: a plug of oakum to keep dry the touchhole of a gun; a plug or *quid* of tobacco; a bar or pin to secure various things (for example, logs); a thatcher's handful of straw; a small, thick piece of anything, including a plug of oakum for the breech or muzzle of a gun, a plug or quid of tobacco, or a piece of cheese. The Rev. Henry Garrett Newland, in *The Erne: Its Legends and Its Fly-Fishing* (1851), p. 71, describes a trout "already cut into fids five or six inches in length." To *fid* or *fidder* was to fix with a fid ("Rigged the maintopmast and fidded it," logbook of the *Lyell,* 1729, Public Record Office, Ruskin Ave., Kew, London).

Freebooter: Pirate, piratical adventurer.

Gash: Waste, rubbish, particularly uneaten food.

Great cabin: The captain's quarters, the largest cabin in the ship.

Grog: Rum and water.

Guaco: South American plant from which was extracted an alleged cure for snakebite. Also "strongly recommended" in Dr. John Mason Good's *Study of Medicine,* 1822, as "an antidote to hydrophobia."

Guanaco: Here the very large Peruvian sheep, "resembling our deer, but some . . . not less than 13 hands" (John Hawkesworth, *An Account of the Voyages and Discoveries Undertaken by Order of His Present Majesty,* Ministry of Defence Admiralty Library, Old Scotland Yard, London, 1773). More correctly, the South American auchenia huanaco, a kind of wild llama that produces a reddish-brown wool, "whereof hats are made in England," observed Adm. Sir John Narborough in his *Journal,* included in *An Account of Several Late Voyages and Discoveries in the South and North*

(London: Samuel Smith and Benjamin Walford, 1694. Original in the Bodleian Library, Oxford, England). Sir John sailed to the South Seas in September 1670 in the three-hundred-ton *Sweepstakes,* had a dispute with the Spaniards in Valdivia, and left two officers and a seaman in their hands when he returned to England in June 1671.

Guano: "Cormorants' dung," according to Shelvocke, but in fact the excrement of sea fowls, including the cormorant and the alcatraces gull, which nested on islands off the Peruvian coast. Also a name for these birds themselves—Spanish *guanae.* Used extensively as a fertilizer. In 1844, Emerson was recommending "a teaspoonful of guano to turn sandbank into corn," and in that year more than three hundred ships from Liverpool alone were in the Spanish guano trade. In 1851, guano water was guaranteed for the health of plants and the color of flowers. Disraeli in his novel *Tancred* (1847) wrote of "Lady Constance having guanoed her mind by reading French novels . . ." Also applied to fertilizer made from fish skins, heads, and bones.

Guayava: Citrus fruit of the guava tree, sharp and sweet in taste, similar to a lime.

Gunwale: Square-sectioned strip of wood around the top of a ship's or boat's side. Pronounced "gunnel."

Hawse: Space between the head of an anchored vessel and her anchors, or the situation of the cables before a ship's stem when moored with two anchors out from forward, one on the starboard, one on the port bow. In modern ships, part of a ship's bow in which channels are cut for anchor cables.

Heel: After end of a ship's keel.

Jerked beef: Beef cured by cutting long slices and drying in the sun. From Peruvian Spanish *charque.*

League: A distance of about three miles.

Letter of marque: A royal or government license to fit out an armed vessel and operate it to capture enemy merchant shipping. See *privateer.*

Middle watch: In the Royal Navy, the twenty-four-hour day is divided into seven watches:

000–0400 (midnight–4:00 A.M.), middle watch
0400–0800 (4:00 A.M.–8:00 A.M.), morning watch
0800–1200 (8:00 A.M.–noon), forenoon watch

1200–1600 (noon–4:00 P.M.), afternoon watch
1600–1800 (4:00 A.M.–6:00 P.M.), first dog watch
1800–2000 (6:00 P.M.–8:00 P.M.), last dog watch
2000–0000 (8:00 P.M.–midnight), first watch

The purpose of the two dog watches was to make an odd number of watches in the twenty-four hours, thus giving the men different watches each day.

Mizzen: Aftermost mast of a three-masted sailing ship.

Moidore: Portuguese gold coin, current in England in the early eighteenth century, worth about twenty-seven shillings. Later became the name for a sum of twenty-seven to twenty-eight shillings. From Latin *moeda* (money) and *aurum* (gold), via old French *moeda d'ouro.* There were many currencies circulating throughout different countries at this time, and no one currency dominated the economic world.

Pappas: Herb with curved leaves similar to those of the cabbage lettuce, used in salads.

Piece of eight: The seventeenth and eighteenth centuries' Spanish dollar, worth eight reales and slightly less than the similar-sized British crown. Worth about 22½ pence today. Early versions were in glittering Peruvian silver on blanks roughly cut from bars, but in the eighteenth century, proper mints opened in Mexico, Guatemala, Peru, and Colombia. The best-known type was the pillar dollar, one side of which was embossed with the two tall Pillars of Hercules, Spanish gateway to the Mediterranean, topped by a crown. The other side bore the Spanish royal coat of arms and the inscription in Latin, "By the Grace of God King of Spain and the Indies."

Pig: Oblong mass of metal from a smelting furnace.

Pink: Dutch *pyncke,* French *pynke,* Italian *pinco.* Mainly a small, full-rigged seagoing or coastal merchant ship, often armed and flat-bottomed, with bulging sides making boarding difficult and a long, narrow, overhanging stern. The latter made quarter-mounted guns more effective. The name was given to a variety of vessels, including: Roger Ascham's sixteenth-century "lytle pinkes" that "in Winter and rough weather . . . forsake the sea" (*Oxford English Dictionary,* compact edition, Oxford University Press, 1971); a small Danish warship; a Dutch herring boat from

Scheveningen; a ten-ton English brig of 1759; a Revenue pink of 1803; a sixty-five-ton schooner of 1861; a very narrow "pinkstern" boat in the Severn; and the well-known old *Liberty and Property* collier of 1890, the last of her race.

Pinks were used as Royal Navy store and hospital ships and could be as large as two hundred tons, as in the case mentioned, or even four hundred tons, and were frequently used to transport masts. The pink proper was fully rigged on three masts, with the Mediterranean pink a lateen-rigged craft similar to a xebec, except in its flat bottom and taller masts. A derivative of the Danish pink was the schooner-rigged *pinky,* one of the oldest types of New England fishing boat, with a Baltic-type hull and a pink stern.

Pinnace: In a ship of this period, the pinnace and launch were her largest boats, with the former the larger of the two.

Piragua: Also known as pirogue, piragoua, periogua, peraouga, perriaga, periauger, perriagoe, perriawger, perioqua, periaqua, periago, oager, and other names. A long, narrow dugout canoe hollowed from the trunk of a single tree. Sometimes deepened by the addition of planks along the sides, or widened by being built of two curved sections with a flat bottom inserted between them. Originally found in the Caribbean and Gulf of Mexico, with versions spreading to Continental and South America. The *Oxford English Dictionary* (compact edition, Oxford University Press, 1971) quotes numerous mentions of the vessel: "Our craft was but canoes and petty oagers" (William Dampier, *Voyage Round the World,* vol. 3, 1697); "To make myself a canoe or periogua" (Daniel Defoe, *The Life and Strange Surprising Adventures of Robinson Crusoe,* 1719, p. 149); "Major Church and his forces were coming against them with twenty-four peraougers, meaning whale-boats" (Benjamin Church, *History of Philip's War,* vol. 2, 1726, p. 127); "A large new perriagua of about thirty-one foot in length" (*New Jersey Architect,* vol. 11, 1733, p. 311); "These perriaguas are long flat-bottomed boats carrying from twenty-five to thirty tons. They have a kind of forecastle and a cabin, but the rest open and no deck. They have two masts and sails like schooners. They row generally with two oars only" (Francis Moore, *Voyage to Georgia,* 1744, p. 49); "two perriougres" (F. H. Hough, *Siege of Detroit,* 1765, p. 115); "The perioqua rapidly approached" (Capt. Frederick Marryat,

Phantom Ship, 1839, p. 27); "The canoes or piroquas of the enemy" (Prescott, *Mexico,* vol. 6, p. 367); "The periagua is a strange rough boat" (Charles Darwin, *Voyage of the Beagle,* 1865, p. 294).

The Louisiana pirogue was a direct descendant of the old West Indian boat. Made from hollowed-out cyprus logs, it was used in swamps and bayous around New Orleans. The Senegal version was a very large canoe used by natives of that region for loading and unloading ships through the heavy surf, sometimes manned by as many as thirty-two paddlers, who showed their paces in annual regattas. The Tahitian model was sometimes fitted with an inverted triangular sail.

Pistole: Spanish gold coin worth about eighteen shillings in English money.

Pooping: "A ship or boat is said to be pooped when a heavy sea comes inboard over the stern or when a ship is in any way damaged or rendered unmanageable through the action of such a sea over the stern." (*Royal Naval Manual of Seamanship,* Vol. 1. London: Her Majesty's Stationery Office, 1937).

Privateer: Armed vessel owned and officered by private persons holding a commission from the government, and authorized to use it against a hostile nation, especially in the capture of merchant shipping. See *letter of marque.*

Pusser's dirk: Dagger carried by midshipmen, supplied by "Pusser's" (purser's) stores.

Roundshot: Cannonball, that is, spherical iron ball for the smooth-bore cannon of the period.

Rove: Past tense of *reeve,* to pass a rope or wire through (a ring), around (a capstan, barrel, bollard), or to make fast to (spar, mast). From the Dutch *reven.*

Scarbots: From French *scurbot,* scurvy. The disease is caused by lack of vitamin C, contained in fresh fruit and greens, often unobtainable at sea in the days of sail. The provision of lime juice in British ships to combat scurvy led to the American word *limey.* Symptoms include bleeding under the skin, loose teeth, and soft gums.

Seventy-four: A seventy-four-gun warship.

Shallop: A light, open boat. From French *chaloupe.*

Spritsail: Square sail, rigged on the bowsprit yard.

Stays, in: Caught without wind when changing from one tack to another.

Tahel (tael): Not a coin, but any of various units of weight in silver once used in Southeast Asia for large transactions. Equivalent to 1.33 ounces (37.6 grams), in 1720 worth about 6 shillings and sixpence (16 pounds, 67 pence today). Dollars and the center-holed "cash" coins were used for small change and minor deals.

Topsail: Sail above the mainsail (main course) and below the topgallant and royal sail on a three-masted sailing ship.

Select Bibliography

Autobiographies, Memoirs, and Firsthand Accounts

Betagh, William. *A Voyage Round the World.* London: T. Combes, 1725.

Cooke, Capt. Edward. *A Voyage to the South Sea.* London: B. Lintot and R. Gosling, 1712.

Frezier, A. F. *Voyage to the South Sea and Along the Coasts of Chili and Peru.* London: Self-published, 1706.

Pepys, Samuel. *Memoirs Relating to the State of the Royal Navy in England for Ten Years.* London: Self-published, 1690. Caird Library, National Maritime Museum, Greenwich, London.

———. *The Diary of Samuel Pepys.* Ed. Lord Braybrooke. London: Frederick Warne, 1903.

Rogers, Capt. Woodes. *A Cruising Voyage Round the World.* London: Self-published, 1712. Caird Library, London.

———. *Life Aboard a British Privateer in the Time of Queen Anne.* Ed. Robert C. Leslie. London: Blackie, 1894.

Shelvocke, Capt. George. *A Voyage Round the World by Way of the Great South Sea.* London: J. Senex, 1726.

———. *Cruise on the Spaniards with His Majesty's Commission.* London: J. Senex, 1724.

Taylor, George, chief mate, *Success. Journal.* Ministry of Defence Admiralty Library, Old Scotland Yard, London.

Other Books

Cabal, Juan. *Piracy and Pirates.* Trans. James Clough. London: Jarrolds, 1957.

Chapin, Howard Millar. *Privateer Ships and Sailors.* Toulon: G. Mouton, 1926.

Chatterton, Edward Keble. *The Romance of Piracy.* London: Seeley Service, 1914.

Collingwood, Harry. *The Log of a Privateersman.* London: Blackie, 1897.

Daupie, Capt. W. *Dampier's Voyages.* Ed. John Masefield. London: E. Grant Richards, 1906.

Feiling, Keith. *A History of England.* London: Book Club Associates, 1972.

Fisher, James. *Bird Recognition.* Vol. 1: *Sea Birds and Waders.* London: Penguin Books, 1947.

Forbes, Rosita. *Sir Henry Morgan: Pirate and Pioneer.* London: Cassell, 1948.

Goodwin, Peter. *The Construction and Fitting of the English Man-of-War, 1630–1830.* Annapolis, Md.: Naval Institute Press, 1987.

Harland, John. *Seamanship in the Age of Sail.* Annapolis, Md.: Naval Institute Press, 1984.

Howell, John. *The Story of Alexander Selkirk.* London: Oliver and Boyd, 1829.

Kinder, Hermann, and Werner Hilgemann. Trans. Ernest A. Meuze. *The Penguin Atlas of World History.* London: Penguin Books, 1986.

Lees, James. *The Masting and Rigging of English Ships of War, 1625–1860.* Annapolis, Md.: Naval Institute Press, 1984.

Lloyd, Christopher. *William Dampier.* London: Faber and Faber, 1966.

Lubbock, Basil. *Bully Hayes, South Sea Pirate.* Boston: Chas. E. Lauriat, 1931.

Marryat, Capt. Frederick. *The Privateersman.* London: Bohn, 1862.

Masefield, John. *On the Spanish Main.* London: Seeley Service, 1906.

McDougall, Walter A. *Let the Sea Make a Noise.* New York: Harper Collins, 1993.

Natkiel, Richard, and Anthony Preston. *Atlas of Maritime History.* London: Weidenfeld and Nicholson, 1986.

Nicholettes, Capt. R. B. *Bristol Privateers of the Eighteenth Century.* London: United Services Magazine, 1898.

O'Brian, Patrick. *Master and Commander.* London: Harper Collins, 1994.

Pack, Capt. James. *Nelson's Blood: The Story of Naval Rum.* Annapolis, Md.: Naval Institute Press, 1996.

Russell, W. Clark. *William Dampier.* London: MacMillan, 1889.

Statham, Comdr. Edward Phillips. *Privateers and Privateering.* London: Hutchinson, 1910.

Stockton, Frank R. *Buccaneers and Pirates of Our Coasts.* New York: Grosset and Dunlap, 1898.

Symons, Henry. *The Taunton Castle Privateer.* London: Proceedings of the Somerset Archaeological and Natural History Society. Vol. 16, part 2, 1910, 136–142.

Tuck, Gerald S. *A Guide to Seabirds on the Ocean Routes.* London: Collins, 1965.

Van Loon, Hendrik Willem. *Ships.* London: Harrup, 1935.

Watts, Anthony J. *The Royal Navy.* Annapolis, Md.: Naval Institute Press, 1995.

Wilkinson, Clennell. *William Dampier.* London: John Lane the Bodley Head, 1929.

Winston, Alexander. *No Purchase, No Pay.* London: Eyre and Spottiswood, 1970.

Wycherley, George. *Buccaneers of the Pacific.* Indianapolis: Bobbs-Merrill, 1928.

Index

About the Author

Kenneth Poolman, whose father served in submarines in World War I and cruisers in World War II, himself spent 1943–46 in minesweepers, destroyers, and aircraft carriers. When he returned to civilian life he attended Cambridge University and eventually worked for the BBC as a writer/producer of documentaries for radio and as a script editor for television.

He has twenty-three books published, mostly on air-sea warfare in World War II. He is also the author of radio and television scripts and many articles on maritime and air warfare. His first book, *The Kelly* (a history of Earl Mountbatten's wartime destroyer command), was commissioned after a radio feature program for the BBC.

The Naval Institute Press is the book-publishing arm of the U.S. Naval Institute, a private, nonprofit, membership society for sea service professionals and others who share an interest in naval and maritime affairs. Established in 1873 at the U.S. Naval Academy in Annapolis, Maryland, where its offices remain today, the Naval Institute has members worldwide.

Members of the Naval Institute support the education programs of the society and receive the influential monthly magazine *Proceedings* and discounts on fine nautical prints and on ship and aircraft photos. They also have access to the transcripts of the Institute's Oral History Program and get discounted admission to any of the Institute-sponsored seminars offered around the country.

The Naval Institute also publishes *Naval History* magazine. This colorful bimonthly is filled with entertaining and thought-provoking articles, first-person reminiscences, and dramatic art and photography. Members receive a discount on *Naval History* subscriptions.

The Naval Institute's book-publishing program, begun in 1898 with basic guides to naval practices, has broadened its scope in recent years to include books of more general interest. Now the Naval Institute Press publishes about one hundred titles each year, ranging from how-to books on boating and navigation to battle histories, biographies, ship and aircraft guides, and novels. Institute members receive discounts of 20 to 50 percent on the Press's nearly six hundred books in print.

Full-time students are eligible for special half-price membership rates. Life memberships are also available.

For a free catalog describing Naval Institute Press books currently available, and for further information about subscribing to *Naval History* magazine or about joining the U.S. Naval Institute, please write to:

Membership Department
U.S. Naval Institute
291 Wood Road
Annapolis, MD 21402-5035
Telephone: (800) 233-8764
Fax: (410) 269-7940
Web address: www.usni.org